A LIFE

THE JOURNEY

A LIFE TRANSFORMED BY GRACE

THE JOURNEY

"A LIFE TRANSFORMED BY GRACE"

PUBLISHED BY:

Michael McCullough

THE JOURNEY

Copyright © 2024   All rights reserved.

This book, or any portion thereof, may not be reproduced, distributed, or transmitted in any form or by any means without the express written consent of the copyright holder, except for brief quotations in book reviews and certain other noncommercial uses permitted by copyright law.

Disclosure:

This book was created with the support of Creative Writing Coach by ChatGPT, a tool that assisted in refining the writing process. The author used this resource for tasks such as research, drafting, and ensuring correct spelling and punctuation, which helped bring the creative vision to life more efficiently.

While the software streamlined certain aspects of production, the author maintained full control over the content, including interpretations, theological perspectives, and conclusions. Creative Writing Coach served primarily to improve efficiency and coherence while preserving the integrity of the author's work.

The integration of AI was thoughtfully managed to ensure the book's core message and essence reflect the author's personal insights. This disclosure is provided in the interest of transparency regarding the use of innovative tools, while affirming that the book's insights, vision, and spiritual depth are fully aligned with the author's commitment to delivering a meaningful and engaging reader experience.

THE JOURNEY

Table of Contents

Introduction: What If There's More? 1
Chapter One: Nowhere Fast, ... 7
Chapter Two: Awakened by Grace 13
Chapter Three: The Divine Invitation 21
Chapter Four: Conviction, ... 27
Chapter Five: The Veil Lifted, ... 33
Chapter Six: From Resistance to Receptivity 39
Chapter Seven: When Faith Finds Its Spark 45
Chapter Eight: Turning Toward the Light, ... 51
Chapter Nine : A New Birth of Hope 57
Chapter Ten: Freedom to Choose, ... 65
Chapter Eleven: Entering the Family of God 81
Chapter Twelve: Baptism, ... 89
Chapter Thirteen: Growth After Grace, ... 97
Chapter Fourteen: Living in the Power of the Spirit 105
Chapter Fifteen: Transformed Desires, ... 111
Chapter Sixteen: Overcoming Trials, ... 119
Chapter Seventeen: Bearing Fruit, ... 129
Chapter Eighteen: The Mission, ... 137
Chapter Nineteen: Strengthened in Service 143
Chapter Twenty: Standing Firm in the Truth 149
Chapter Twenty-One: Kingdom Mindset 155
Chapter Twenty-Two: A Witness to the World 161
Chapter Twenty-Three: Walking Together, ... 167
Chapter Twenty-Four: The Journey, ... 175
Chapter Twenty-Five: The Journey Continues 179

THE JOURNEY

Introduction: What If There's More?

Have you ever felt like life is just too much—like no matter how hard you try, the weight keeps pressing down, and nothing you do seems to lift it? Maybe you're caught in the grind of endless to-do lists, work demands, and bills that keep piling up. Maybe you find yourself scrolling through social media late at night, looking for something to fill the void, only to feel more disconnected and empty than before. Or perhaps it's something deeper—an ache in your soul, a quiet but constant emptiness that lingers even when you're surrounded by friends and loved ones.

You've tried to outrun it. You've chased happiness, purpose, and a reason to keep going. You've poured yourself into relationships, achievements, and distractions. And yet, no matter what you do, it still feels like something is missing. Like it's not enough.

If that sounds familiar, I want you to know something: you're not alone. And even more importantly, you don't have to stay stuck in that place.

I don't say that lightly. I know what it's like to feel weighed down. I've been there too.

For years, I carried an invisible burden—a heaviness that I couldn't shake. On the outside, my life looked fine. I stayed busy, threw myself into work, relationships, and hobbies, and followed all the usual advice about how to be happy. But inside, I was restless. No matter how much I accomplished or how hard I worked, I couldn't fill the emptiness I felt. It was like chasing the wind—always running, always searching, but never finding the peace I longed for.

What I didn't realize at the time was that I was stuck in a cycle I couldn't break on my own. The more I tried to fix myself, the more tangled and exhausted I became. I convinced myself that if I could just do more, achieve more, or find the next big thing, I'd finally feel whole. But every effort left me more drained, more overwhelmed, and more lost.

Maybe you've felt something similar. Maybe you've found yourself asking the same questions I did: Is this all there is? Why does life feel so heavy? Why can't I find what I'm looking for?

Here's what I've learned: when you hit that point—when you feel like you've reached the end of yourself—it doesn't have to be the end of the story. In fact, it might just be the beginning of something new.

There's something powerful about being in a place where you've run out of your own strength. It's in those moments, when all your usual solutions stop working, that you're finally open to something greater.

What if I told you that life doesn't have to feel this heavy? That you don't have to carry the weight on your own? What if I told you that peace, hope, and purpose are not only possible, but they're closer than you think?

That's where grace comes in.

Grace isn't about fixing yourself or pretending you've got it all together. It's not about being perfect or following a list of rules. Grace meets you exactly where you are—in the mess, in the questions, in the heaviness you're feeling right now. Grace says you don't have to have all the answers, and you don't have to clean yourself up before you take the next step. Grace is a gift, freely given, and all you have to do is receive it.

I don't know where you are in your journey. Maybe you believe in God but feel disconnected from Him. Maybe you've been hurt by religion or feel like faith is just another burden to carry. Maybe you're skeptical, unsure if any of this is real, or if it could possibly apply to you.

Whatever your story is, I want you to know this: grace is for you.

It's for the one who feels like they've failed too many times.

It's for the one who's tired of putting on a brave face.

It's for the one who feels stuck, lost, or too far gone.

Grace doesn't look at where you've been—it looks at where you can go.

Over the course of this book, I've shared my journey of faith—not because my story is extraordinary, but because it's a testimony to the extraordinary grace of God. It's a journey that began in brokenness and restlessness, but step by step, God met me in my struggles and transformed my life.

We start this journey with me at 18 years of age, fresh out of high school, restless and searching for something I couldn't quite define. Back then, I was like so many others my age—standing at the edge of adulthood with no real sense of where I was headed. My days were filled with the usual distractions: hanging out with friends, dreaming big dreams that felt distant and vague, and trying to figure out what life was supposed to look like. There was a void in my heart that I couldn't quite put into words, but I didn't understand it at the time. I only knew that something was missing.

Through the pages that followed, I've reflected on the moments that shaped me: meeting Joy, the woman who became my wife and partner in faith; the times when God stretched me through mission trips and accountability relationships; and the slow, steady process of learning to trust Him in every season.

I've also shared the lessons God has taught me along the way—lessons about grace, forgiveness, and the importance of community. I've written about the call to make disciples, the power of love, and the beauty of leaving a legacy of faith for the next generation. And through it all, one truth has echoed louder than any other: God is faithful.

And now as I look back at my journey, I can say with confidence that the same grace that transformed my life is available to you. You don't have to carry your burdens alone. You don't have to fix yourself before you take the first step. Grace meets you where you are and walks with you into something new.

So let me ask you:

Are you tired of carrying the weight on your own?

Are you ready to take just one step toward hope, healing, and purpose?

Are you willing to ask the question: What if there's more?

This book isn't about giving you all the answers. It's not a formula or a checklist for how to live a perfect life. It's an invitation—to explore, to question, and to discover what grace could mean for you.

Because here's the truth: you don't have to have it all figured out. You don't have to fix everything overnight. All you need is the courage to say, What if?

What if God is real?

What if hope is possible for me?

What if there's more to life than this?

The same grace that met me is reaching out to you right now. No matter where you've been, no matter how heavy life feels, hope is closer than you think.

So, if you're ready to take that first step, let's walk this journey together. You don't have to do it alone.

Grace is waiting. Are you ready to receive it?

Chapter One: Nowhere Fast, When Hope Feels Out of Reach

Have you ever felt like your life was one long series of escape attempts?

Like no matter how far you went or how many fresh starts you tried to build, you kept circling back to the same version of yourself—the one you were running from? For years, that's exactly how I lived. Every move, every decision, every bold proclamation that I was finally going to turn over a new leaf ended the same way: me, staring into the mirror, unable to escape the hollow, tired look in my own eyes.

By the end of the summer of 1979, I was 18 years old and already drowning in a mess of my own making. Life in the suburbs felt suffocating, like I was caught in a loop I couldn't break. My days were consumed with drug use, heavy drinking, and petty crime. It wasn't an accident or an unfortunate twist of fate—I had built this chaos brick by brick, bad choice by bad choice. Back then, though, I didn't see it as a problem. It was just life on the streets. This was how things were. Everyone I spent time with was just as reckless, and I thought this was all there was.

But something inside me began to shift as the days blurred together in a haze of substances, parties, and bad decisions. There was a quiet discomfort that I couldn't ignore, a small, gnawing whisper deep inside that said, This isn't it. There's more to life than this. I didn't know what to do with that feeling, so I tried to silence it. I drank more, smoked more, partied harder. But no matter how loud the noise around me got, the whisper only grew louder.

It wasn't guilt—not yet—but it was something close to it. A heaviness. A weight pressing down on my chest, making it harder and harder to pretend that my life wasn't falling apart. I was exhausted—not just physically, but emotionally and spiritually. I was tired of pretending to be fine, tired of filling myself with things that didn't satisfy, tired of trying to keep up with people who seemed just as lost as I was.

I knew I needed to get out of Michigan. In my mind, the problem wasn't me—it was the people around me, the places I spent my time, the reputation I had built for myself. If I could just leave, I thought, everything would get better. I convinced myself that I could start over somewhere new, that I could leave all the bad choices, the mistakes, and the emptiness behind me, like garbage tossed out the window on the highway.

When two of my party buddies mentioned they were moving to Houston, Texas, it felt like my way out. The economy in Michigan was a disaster at the time—jobs were scarce, and there was little hope of anything changing. But Houston was different. My friends talked about it like it was a city of endless opportunity, a place where you could reinvent yourself. They offered me a seat in their car if I could pitch in for gas money. I didn't have to think twice. This was my chance, and I grabbed it with both hands.

The drive south was filled with hope for me, or at least what I thought was hope. I spent hours staring out the window, imagining how different my life was going to be once we arrived. In my head, Texas wasn't just another state—it was a new beginning. I pictured myself finding a job, meeting new people, and leaving behind all the mistakes I'd made in Michigan. I thought I could shed my past like an old skin and finally be free of the person I had been.

For a while, it seemed like it was working. Houston was bustling, a city full of energy and possibilities. I found a job quickly, stayed busy, and tried to convince myself that I had left my old ways behind. For a few months, I almost believed it. But here's the thing about running: no matter how far you go, you can't outrun yourself.

It started small. A drink here, a party there. Little compromises I told myself were harmless. I was still in control, or at least that's what I kept telling myself. But control is a slippery thing, and before I knew it, the old patterns were back. The faces around me were different, the city was new, but the emptiness inside me hadn't gone anywhere. It didn't take long before I was back to the same cycle I had been trapped in back in Michigan—drinking too much, making bad decisions, and trying to fill the void with things that never lasted.

I remember one night in particular. I was standing in front of the cracked mirror in the tiny apartment I shared with my friends. The reflection staring back at me looked hollow and defeated. I hated that face. I hated the choices I'd made, hated the person I had become. And for the first time, I stopped blaming Michigan.

The truth hit me like a punch to the gut: the problem wasn't the people I had left behind, or the city I had run away from. The problem was me. And no matter how far I ran, no matter how many times I tried to start over, I couldn't escape myself.

That realization was terrifying. It felt like there was no way out. I had tried to fix my life on my own, and I had failed. I had tried running, and I had failed. Everywhere I went, the same problems followed me because I was carrying them inside me. I didn't know how to change, and I was scared that I never would.

By the time I hit my breaking point, I was now 21 years old. Three years had passed since I'd left Michigan, and I was no better off than when I'd started. If anything, I was worse. I had run out of excuses, run out of distractions, and run out of hope. That's when I picked up the phone and called my father.

I didn't know what I was going to say when he answered. I didn't have a plan. I just knew I couldn't keep going like I was. For so long, I had kept my struggles to myself, too proud to admit that I didn't have it all together. But something broke in me that day. My walls came down, and for the first time, I let myself say it out loud: "Dad, I don't know what to do anymore."

There was a pause on the other end of the line. Not an awkward pause, but the kind of pause that comes from someone who knows you better than you know yourself and is waiting for you to get there on your own. When he finally spoke, his voice was calm, steady, and full of love: "Meet me halfway, son. Come to your aunt's place in Tennessee, and we'll figure it out together."

It wasn't what I expected him to say. I thought he might lecture me, or try to tell me how to fix my life. Instead, he offered me an escape route. A lifeline. He didn't ask for explanations or demand that I clean myself up first. He just offered me a way out.

Looking back now, I can see what he was really doing. He wasn't just offering me a place to stay—he was rescuing me. He was pulling me out of the toxic environment I had surrounded myself with and giving me a chance to breathe again. At the time, I couldn't see that. All I knew was that I had nowhere else to turn, and his offer felt like the only light in a very dark place.

Leaving Houston wasn't easy. It felt like admitting failure. I had gone to Texas hoping to prove that I could rebuild my life on my own, and walking away felt like admitting that I couldn't. But deep down, I knew the truth: I couldn't do it alone.

The flight to Tennessee felt like a journey in more ways than one. With every mile, I felt a little more of the weight I'd been carrying begin to lift. I didn't know what was waiting for me when I got there, but I knew it had to be better than the life I was leaving behind. For the first time in years, I felt a flicker of hope. It was small, fragile, and easy to overlook, but it was there—a quiet whisper that said, Maybe things can be different.

When I arrived at the airport in Knoxville, my father was waiting for me. He hugged me, and for the first time in what felt like forever, I didn't feel like I had to pretend to be okay. My cousin had come with him to pick me up, and when I climbed into their car, I felt something I hadn't felt in years: safe.

Tennessee became the place where everything started to change. It wasn't instant, and it wasn't easy, but it was the first step on a journey that would change my life forever. It was where the running stopped, where the fog began to lift, and where I started to believe that maybe—just maybe—there was still hope for someone like me.

Chapter Two: Awakened by Grace

Have you ever had a moment that completely rewrote the script of your life?

Not just a fleeting thought or a moment of doubt, but a deep, soul-shaking experience that forced you to stop and take a hard look at the road you were on. Maybe it wasn't loud or dramatic—no sirens blaring or skies opening up. Maybe it came quietly, like a whisper you couldn't ignore anymore, or like the weight of silence settling over you after years of distractions. Or maybe it was something big—a loss so profound it shattered the illusion you'd been clinging to. Whatever it was, it left you stripped bare, asking questions you'd been too scared to face before. Questions like:

Is this all there is? Why does it feel like I'm going nowhere? Does my life actually mean anything?

For some, these moments creep in slowly, like a gentle tap on the shoulder, a quiet reminder that something is missing. For others, they crash in like a tidal wave, knocking you off your feet and leaving you gasping for air. Either way, they have a way of exposing the truth we work so hard to avoid. The truth that something isn't right. That something inside us is broken. That something is missing.

One particular Sunday morning in Tennessee was my moment.

Just months earlier, I had fled Houston with nothing but a carry-on bag and the last flicker of hope I could muster. Life in Texas had unraveled completely—years of bad choices and broken habits had caught up to me, and I found myself suffocating under the weight of my own mess. When I finally called my father and admitted I didn't know what to do anymore, his response was simple but life-changing: "Meet me halfway. Come to Tennessee, and we'll figure it out together."

I packed up, left behind the wreckage I'd created, and stepped onto that plane with no idea what the future held. I didn't know what I was looking for; I just knew I couldn't keep living the way I was. I hoped Tennessee would be different. I hoped it would be enough to quiet the ache inside me.

When I arrived, life settled into something slower, something simpler. My aunt welcomed me into her home with open arms and a kind of love I hadn't felt in years. My cousin, just a year older than me, quickly became my partner in this attempt at a fresh start. Our days were spent fishing in quiet streams, hunting in the Tennessee woods, or working on his beat-up Pontiac Tempest—a car that seemed like it was always one bad day away from falling apart completely. It was peaceful, almost therapeutic. The chaos of Houston felt like a distant memory, and I convinced myself that this change of scenery would be enough to make everything better.

But even in the stillness of Tennessee, something wasn't right. The emptiness I'd been carrying for years hadn't disappeared. It was quieter now, hidden beneath the surface, but it was still there—a persistent ache in the background of my life. It whispered to me in the quiet moments, reminding me that no matter how far I'd run, I hadn't outrun myself. I was still the same broken person inside, no matter where I lived or how much I tried to distract myself.

My aunt, a kind but no-nonsense woman, had one specific rule: if you lived under her roof, you went to church on Sunday. No arguments. No exceptions. I wasn't thrilled about it, but I figured it was a small price to pay for the fresh start she had given me. So every Sunday morning, I went. I didn't complain—not out loud, anyway—but I made sure everyone, including myself, knew that I wasn't really there for "church."

Every week, I slipped into the back row of the pews, as close to the exit as I could get without drawing attention. I crossed my arms, stared at the floor, and counted the minutes until the service was over and I could bolt out the door within seconds of that last amen. I didn't sing. I didn't bow my head in prayer. I didn't even pretend to listen. I was just there to fulfill my obligation, to check the box so I could say I'd done it. I thought I was doing her a favor just by showing up.

And then one Sunday, everything changed.

It started out like any other service. The preacher stood at the pulpit, delivering his sermon with the same energy he brought every week. I wasn't paying attention at first, lost in my own thoughts, counting the minutes as usual. But then something he said caught my attention. He started talking about the weight we carry when we try to live life on our own terms—the heaviness that comes from chasing after things that were never meant to satisfy us. He described how we fill our lives with temporary fixes—money, relationships, success, distractions—all in an attempt to quiet the ache inside us, only to find ourselves emptier than before.

It was like he had been following me around, like he had read my story and was retelling it to the whole congregation. Every word he spoke felt like it was aimed directly at me, peeling back the layers I had spent years building up. He wasn't just describing my mistakes—he was describing my heart. My emptiness. My exhaustion. It was like he was holding up a mirror, forcing me to see the truth I'd been running from: I wasn't okay. I wasn't fine. And I couldn't keep pretending I was.

For the first time in years, I couldn't tune it out. I couldn't roll my eyes or brush it off. His words cut through every defense I had built, and I felt something stir inside me—something I couldn't explain and didn't fully understand at the time. It wasn't guilt, exactly. It wasn't shame. It was something softer, something kinder. It was grace.

Grace. The preacher described it as a gift—something unearned, undeserved, freely given. He said grace meets us exactly where we are, no matter how messy or broken or lost we might feel. He said grace doesn't wait for us to fix ourselves first; it comes to us in the middle of our chaos and offers us a way out. A way forward.

Of course, I had heard the word "grace" before, but it had always felt distant, abstract—like something meant for other people, people better than me. But that morning, grace felt real. It felt personal. And for the first time, I wondered if it could be meant for me, too.

When the preacher invited anyone who was tired of carrying their burdens to come forward and pray, I froze. My heart was racing. My chest felt tight. My hands gripped the edge of the pew so hard my knuckles turned white. My mind was screaming at me to stay put. This isn't for you. You're fine. You don't need this.

But my heart knew better. I wasn't fine. I was tired. Tired of pretending. Tired of running. Tired of carrying the weight of my choices alone. I didn't know what was waiting for me at the altar, but I knew I couldn't stay where I was. I needed something—anything—to change.

Before I realized what I was doing, I stood up. My legs felt like they weighed a thousand pounds, but somehow they kept moving. I stepped into the aisle, fully aware of the eyes of the congregation on me, but too desperate to care. Each step felt heavier than the last, like I was walking through mud. When I finally reached the altar, I dropped to my knees.

And for the first time in my life, I stopped pretending.

I let my guard down, and everything I had been carrying for so long poured out of me. The guilt. The shame. The exhaustion. The fear that I would never be enough. I didn't have the right words to pray. I didn't even know if I was doing it "right." I just begged God for help. For forgiveness. For something—anything—to change.

In the stillness that followed, something incredible happened.

It wasn't loud or dramatic. There were no flashing lights or booming voices. It was quiet, like a whisper that settled over my heart. But it was undeniable. In that moment, I felt something lift. The weight I had been carrying for so long was gone. And in its place, there was peace. A peace I had never known before. It wasn't just a feeling—it was a knowing. A knowing that I wasn't alone anymore. A knowing that I didn't have to carry everything by myself. A knowing that God had been waiting for me all along, even when I hadn't been looking for Him.

That was grace.

It didn't fix everything overnight. My life didn't magically transform in an instant. But something inside me changed that day. For the first time in years, I felt hope. Real hope. The kind that whispers, Maybe things can be different. Maybe I don't have to stay the way I am.

That moment at the altar was the beginning of a new chapter. It was the moment I stopped running and started letting grace lead the way. I didn't have all the answers, and I still had a long road ahead. But I knew one thing for certain: I didn't have to walk that road alone. And for the first time in a long time, that was enough.

THE JOURNEY

Chapter Three: The Divine Invitation

I didn't fully grasp the enormity of what had happened to me that Sunday morning—not immediately, at least. Something had undeniably changed, like a switch flipped deep inside my soul, but I couldn't put it into words yet. All I knew was that the weight I had carried for so long—the guilt, the shame, the restlessness—had been lifted. It was as if I had been drowning for years and, for the first time, my head broke the surface. I could breathe again. For the first time in years, there was a flicker of hope where there had only been numbness.

But as the emotional high of that moment began to settle into the quietness of the days that followed, I found myself asking a question that refused to let go of me: What now?

I had encountered grace in a way I couldn't deny. I had felt something I had never felt before—a peace that seemed to fill the cracks in my heart that nothing else had been able to touch. But grace wasn't a "finish line." It wasn't the end of the story. It was the start of something new, and that terrified me because I didn't know what "new" looked like.

The question still lingered: Now what?

Grace had opened a door for me, but I realized that I had to choose whether or not to walk through it. It wasn't going to drag me forward or shove me into a new life. It wasn't going to demand anything of me. Instead, grace was gently offering an invitation—a divine invitation to walk a new path, not alone, but with God.

And here's what I began to realize: grace isn't a one-time event. It's not just about a single moment where you feel peace or hope. Grace is an unfolding journey, a series of steps that lead you deeper and deeper into something you never thought possible. It's the beginning of a relationship—a partnership—with a God who knows you intimately, loves you unconditionally, and wants to walk alongside you every step of the way.

But like any invitation, it required a response.

For so long, I had tried to do everything on my own. I had tried to fix myself, to outrun my past, to prove that I was strong enough to handle life without any help. And for so long, all of it had failed. Grace was asking me to lay all of that down. It wasn't asking for perfection or promises that I couldn't keep. It was asking for surrender.

That might sound simple, but for me, surrender was the hardest thing in the world. I had spent so many years building up walls around my heart, convincing myself that I didn't need anyone or anything. To open myself up—to admit that I needed help—felt like standing naked in the middle of a crowded room. It felt terrifying.

But something inside me whispered, You don't have to do this alone anymore.

I had spent so long believing the lie that everything was up to me. That my worth was tied to how much I achieved. That I had to carry the weight of my mistakes, my failures, and my pain all by myself. And now, grace was offering me something radically different: freedom.

It wasn't freedom from challenges or struggles. Those things didn't magically disappear. But it was freedom from the lie that I had to face them alone. It was freedom to let go of the crushing pressure to be enough on my own.

The first step in responding to that invitation was trust.

And trust wasn't something that came naturally to me. Trusting people had always been risky, and it had burned me more times than I cared to admit. Trusting God felt even harder. I didn't know how to trust a God I couldn't see; a God I didn't fully understand yet. But what I was starting to learn was that trust didn't mean having all the answers. It didn't mean knowing exactly how everything was going to work out. Trust meant taking one small step forward, even if I couldn't see where the road was leading.

It was a process, not an instant transformation. There were moments when I felt peace and moments when I felt like I was back at square one. There were days when I doubted whether I had really changed at all. But even in those moments, grace never left me. It kept showing up, meeting me exactly where I was—whether I was taking a step forward or stumbling backward.

That's the thing about grace: it's not a reward for getting it right. It's not something you earn by being good enough or doing enough. Grace meets you in your mess, in your brokenness, and invites you to take the next step—not because you deserve it, but because you're loved.

One of the most beautiful things I began to understand about grace is how personal it is. It's not a "one-size-fits-all" solution. God's grace doesn't come to us as a formula or a checklist. It comes to us exactly where we are, speaking directly to the places in our hearts that need healing the most.

For me, grace began with the simple but profound truth that I didn't have to carry the weight of my life on my own anymore. That truth felt like a breath of fresh air after years of suffocating under the pressure to hold everything together. But grace didn't stop there. It kept inviting me deeper, asking me to trust God not just with the big, life-changing moments but with the small, everyday ones too.

Maybe you've felt that gentle nudge before—that quiet tug on your heart that tells you there's more to life than what you've been living. Maybe it's a whisper you've been ignoring, or maybe it's something you've felt for the first time today. If that's you, I want you to know this: God's invitation is for you.

It's not just for people who seem like they have it all together. It's not for the "perfect" or the "religious." It's for you, right here, right now, exactly as you are. You don't have to fix yourself first. You don't have to have all the answers. You don't have to be anything other than who you are in this moment.

Grace isn't about earning God's love—it's about receiving it.

And receiving it doesn't have to be complicated. For me, it started with simple, stumbling prayers—prayers that didn't sound eloquent or polished but came from the depths of my heart. It started with moments of silence, moments of honesty, moments of choosing to believe that maybe—just maybe—God's love was big enough to hold even me.

Maybe for you, it looks like finding a quiet space to reflect or opening a Bible for the first time. Maybe it's as simple as whispering, God, I'm here. I don't know what to do, but I'm here. Whatever it looks like, know this: God is already waiting for you.

The invitation is there, and it's not going anywhere.

God doesn't demand that you clean yourself up before you come to Him. He's not waiting for you to fix all your problems or get your life together first. He's waiting for you, just as you are—with open arms, with grace, and with a love that has no limits.

When I think back to that Sunday morning, to the first moment I felt grace break through my defenses, I realize now that it wasn't the end of the story. It was the beginning. It was the moment God invited me to step into a new way of living—not a perfect life, but a life where I didn't have to walk alone.

And that invitation? It's for you too. Will you open the door?

Chapter Four: Conviction, A Heart Stirred to Life

When I first experienced grace, it felt like stepping into sunlight after years of wandering in darkness. I didn't know how long I had been lost until the light hit me, warming parts of my soul I had forgotten existed. That day at the altar, with tears streaming down my face and a burden I had carried for years suddenly lifted, I felt free for the first time in my life. Free to hope. Free to breathe. Free to believe that maybe—just maybe—I didn't have to keep running.

It was life-changing. For the first time, I truly understood that God's love wasn't something I had to earn. It wasn't dependent on my performance or dictated by the long list of failures I had racked up over the years. It simply was. A love so pure and unrelenting that it met me right in my mess and refused to leave me there.

For a while, I thought that was it—that grace was the end of the story. That moment at the altar had brought me peace, and I assumed the hardest part was behind me. I had been forgiven, hadn't I? What more could there be? But as the days turned into weeks, I began to realize something profound: grace doesn't just save you. It changes you.

At first, I didn't recognize it for what it was. It started quietly, like a faint whisper in the back of my mind: There's more for you than this. Those words would surface in the stillness of the morning, in the quiet moments between activities, or even in the middle of conversations. At first, I brushed them off. I told myself; I've already been forgiven—what else is there to do? But the whisper didn't go away. It grew stronger, clearer, until I couldn't ignore it anymore.

That whisper was conviction.

Conviction isn't something you can easily explain. It's not guilt—it's deeper than that. It's not condemnation—it's gentler than that. Conviction is what happens when God's grace begins to take root in your heart. It's His way of shining a light on the places you've kept hidden, not to shame you, but to heal you. It's His way of saying, I love you just as you are, but I love you too much to leave you here.

For me, conviction felt like God slowly peeling back the layers of my heart, one by one. At first, I resisted. There were things I didn't want to look at—wounds I had buried, habits I had justified, and patterns of thinking I had carried for so long they felt like a part of me. But conviction doesn't let you stay in denial. It's persistent, but it's also patient. It doesn't force its way in. It waits for you to stop running, to stop avoiding, and to say, Okay, God. I'm ready to face this.

The first cracks in my defenses came in the form of small realizations—moments that seemed insignificant at the time but would later reveal the areas where God wanted to work.

I started to notice things about myself that I had ignored for years. The way my frustration would spill out as sharp words, especially toward the people I loved most. The way I used humor or sarcasm as a shield to keep others from seeing the real me. The way I justified selfish decisions with thoughts like, It's not a big deal, or Everyone does it.

One night stands out in my memory. I had gotten into a conversation with a neighbor a couple houses down from my aunts, and in the moment, I let my anger take over and the conversation quickly turned into a heated argument. My words were biting, dismissive, and designed to wound. At the time, I didn't think much of it. But later that evening, as I sat alone replaying the conversation in my mind, something stirred deep within me.

It wasn't the sting of guilt—it was something more profound. It was as if God was gently placing His hand on my shoulder and saying, This isn't who you were created to be.

That realization hit me hard. The argument wasn't just about the words I had said—it was about the condition of my heart. My sharp words weren't random; they came from a place of insecurity and fear that I had ignored for years. And in that moment, I knew God wasn't asking me to fix it on my own. He was inviting me to let Him in, to let Him heal the places I had kept hidden for so long.

Here's what I've come to understand about conviction: it's not about punishment. It's not about God pointing out everything you've done wrong and leaving you to figure it out. Conviction is love in action. It's God saying, I see where you're hurting, and I want to help you heal. I see where you're stuck, and I want to set you free.

But conviction isn't easy. It requires honesty. It requires humility. It requires a willingness to confront the parts of yourself you'd rather avoid. For me, responding to conviction meant taking a hard look at my life and asking God to show me the areas that needed to change. It meant acknowledging that I didn't have it all together and that I couldn't fix myself.

It also meant taking practical steps. I started praying more intentionally—not just for forgiveness, but for transformation. I asked God to help me see people the way He sees them, to soften my words, and to replace my sarcasm with kindness. I began to pause before speaking, especially in moments of frustration, and ask myself, Will these words build someone up or tear them down?

One of the hardest lessons I had to learn was how to apologize. After that argument with the neighbor, I knew I needed to make things right. I picked up the phone, took a deep breath, and humbled myself enough to admit that I had been wrong. It wasn't easy—apologies never are—but it was necessary. And in that moment, I felt a weight lift off my shoulders.

That's the beauty of conviction. It's not about dwelling on past mistakes—it's about giving you the opportunity to move forward in a better way.

As I leaned into the work of conviction, I began to notice changes in myself. They weren't dramatic or immediate, but they were real. My words became softer. My relationships grew deeper. I found myself pausing in moments of frustration, choosing grace over anger.

Conviction didn't just change my behavior—it changed my heart.

If grace is the doorway to a relationship with God, conviction is the path that leads you deeper into that relationship. It's not something to fear—it's something to embrace. Conviction doesn't tear you down. It builds you up. It wakes you up to the life God created you to live.

Maybe you've felt that stirring in your heart—that gentle nudge telling you there's more for you than this. Maybe there's a habit, a relationship, or a mindset God has been asking you to surrender. If that's you, I encourage you: don't run from it. Conviction isn't about punishment—it's about love.

Take a moment to listen. Ask God to show you what He wants to change in your heart, and trust that He will walk with you every step of the way.

You don't have to get it all right. You don't have to have all the answers. You just have to be willing.

Because when you respond to conviction, something beautiful happens. Your heart begins to change. Your perspective shifts. You start to see yourself and others through God's eyes. And slowly but surely, you become the person He created you to be.

That's the thing about grace—it doesn't just save you. It transforms you. One step, one choice, one moment at a time.

Chapter Five: The Veil Lifted, Seeing Truth for the First Time

Conviction isn't a comfortable process. If anything, it's deeply unsettling. It's like someone slowly peeling away the layers of armor you've spent years building, exposing the vulnerable parts of yourself you've worked so hard to protect. And yet, it's also profoundly necessary. Conviction doesn't come to destroy you—it comes to set you free. At the time, I didn't fully understand that. All I knew was that as God worked on my heart, something was changing inside me.

Conviction had shown me where I was stuck, where I was broken, and where I needed to let God in. It felt like He had reached into my soul and flipped on a light switch, illuminating corners of my life I had long ignored. At first, it was uncomfortable—like standing in front of a mirror that reflects not just your face, but everything you've tried to hide. But as that light began to spread, something extraordinary happened: the fog I had been living in started to lift.

It was a gradual process, but it was unmistakable. Little by little, the lies I had believed about myself, about God, and about the world began to lose their grip on me. The patterns of thought that had once felt so permanent, so unshakable, began to crumble under the weight of truth. And as those walls came down, I began to see clearly for the first time in my life.

If I had thought conviction was the end of the process—the difficult step I had to endure before I could move forward—I was wrong. Conviction wasn't the end; it was just another step in the journey. It had cleared away the clutter and distractions, making room for something far greater. It was as if God had been patiently waiting, saying, Now that you've let go of what's holding you back, let me show you what's real.

And what He showed me was nothing short of life-changing.

Have you ever had a moment where something you thought you understood suddenly shifted into focus? Like you'd been looking at a blurry image for so long that you'd convinced yourself it was clear, and then, out of nowhere, everything sharpens? It's disorienting at first. There's a strange mix of clarity and discomfort because you realize how much you weren't seeing before. But it's also exhilarating. It's like stepping out of the shadows and into the light, where you can finally see things as they really are.

That's what happened to me when God began to reveal His truth.

It didn't happen all at once. It wasn't like flipping a switch and suddenly everything was crystal clear. It was more like the slow pulling back of a curtain, one layer at a time. Sometimes it came in quiet, reflective moments—times when I was alone, thinking about the choices I'd made and the life I'd lived. Other times, it hit me like a flood, rushing in with such force that it left me breathless.

Either way, the result was the same. The veil that had clouded my vision for so long began to lift, and for the first time, I could see.

Before that moment, my life felt like driving through a thick fog at night. I could see just far enough ahead to keep going, but I was constantly second-guessing myself. Every turn felt like a gamble. Every step forward felt uncertain. I thought I was doing okay—I thought I could figure it out on my own. But looking back now, I realize the truth: I wasn't okay. I was lost. And I didn't even know it.

The fog that blinded me wasn't made of anything obvious. It wasn't like I was actively rejecting God or denying the truth. It was more subtle than that. My vision was clouded by pride, by distractions, by the endless pursuit of things I thought would bring me happiness. I was so focused on surviving the day-to-day grind that I didn't realize how far I had drifted from anything real.

But God, in His infinite patience, started to open my eyes.

It began with small moments—things I might have overlooked if I wasn't paying attention. A song on the radio that spoke directly to what I was feeling. A conversation with a friend that planted a seed of thought I couldn't shake. I began to reading the Bible, and it actually started to make sense in a ways I had never seen before. Verse after verse would seemingly leap off the page only to take root in my heart.

At first, I dismissed these moments as coincidences. But as they kept happening, I began to wonder: What if this isn't random? What if God is trying to get my attention?

For so long, I had seen God as distant, detached, impersonal. I thought of Him as some faraway being who had set the universe in motion but wasn't particularly interested in the details of my life. But as I began to seek Him, I started to see the truth: God isn't distant. He's personal. He's intimate. He's involved.

I began to understand that He knew me—every fear, every doubt, every struggle. He wasn't just aware of my life; He cared about it. Deeply. And for the first time, I realized that the God I had been running from was the very God who had been pursuing me all along.

As the veil continued to lift, it wasn't just God that I began to see clearly. I also began to see myself.

I started to recognize how much of my life had been shaped by lies—lies I had believed about who I was and what I needed to be happy.

Lies like:

"You have to earn your worth."

"You have to keep everything under control."

"You're on your own in this life."

These lies had driven so many of my decisions. They had dictated how I saw myself, how I interacted with others, and even how I viewed God. But as God's truth began to replace those lies, everything started to shift.

I began to see that my worth wasn't based on what I did, but on who God said I was. I didn't have to carry the weight of the world on my shoulders, because God was the one holding it all together. And I wasn't alone—I never had been.

When the veil is lifted, it changes everything.

It changes the way you see your purpose. It changes the way you see your relationships. It even changes the way you see the little things—the everyday moments that once felt insignificant suddenly become meaningful.

I began to notice beauty in places I had overlooked before. The small, ordinary blessings I used to take for granted—like the laughter of a friend or the quiet stillness of a morning—now felt like gifts. The relationships I had neglected became opportunities to love and serve. And the future I used to fear became an adventure I didn't have to navigate alone.

Living in the light of God's truth doesn't mean life becomes perfect. There are still challenges. There are still moments of doubt. There are still days when the fog threatens to return. But even in those moments, there's a confidence that wasn't there before—a confidence that comes from knowing the One who holds the truth.

Because when God reveals His truth, it's not just about showing you who He is—it's about inviting you to live in that truth.

Seeing the truth was the first step. Surrendering to it would be the next.

Chapter Six: From Resistance to Receptivity

When God began to reveal His truth to me, I felt like a new person. It was as if someone had handed me a key to a door I didn't even know existed—a door to freedom, love, and purpose. For the first time, I began to understand who God truly was and, by extension, who I was in Him. It was a revelation that shattered years of lies I'd believed about myself, about others, and about the world. But as profound as that clarity was, it didn't mean the battle was over. In fact, it was just beginning.

The battle wasn't external anymore. It wasn't about trying to escape my circumstances or outrun my past. The fight was internal now, rooted in the deepest parts of my heart. Even with all the grace and truth God had poured into my life, I found myself holding back, clinging to control over certain areas I wasn't ready to fully surrender.

I used to think surrendering to God was something you did once—a single, definitive act where you gave your life to Him and that was that. But I learned that surrender isn't a one-time decision. It's not a line you cross and never have to revisit. Surrender is daily. It's ongoing. It's a choice you make every morning, every moment, to trust God with all of who you are. And for someone like me, who had spent years relying on no one but myself, that choice didn't come easily.

My natural instinct has always been resistance. Even as a kid, I liked to feel in control—to have a plan, to know what was coming, to steer my own ship. That instinct didn't just disappear when I gave my heart to God. If anything, it became even more apparent, as if my soul was wrestling with the idea of fully letting go.

I didn't resist God outright. I wasn't defiant or openly rebellious. My resistance was quieter, more subtle. It hid in the corners of my mind, wrapped in justifications that sounded reasonable on the surface. I told myself things like:

"I trust God, but I still need to keep my hands on the wheel."

"I'll surrender that part of my life... just not yet."

"What if I let go and everything falls apart?"

That last thought hit me the hardest. What if? It's a question that kept me stuck in fear. I was afraid of what would happen if I let go of the things I was holding onto—my plans, my relationships, my sense of control. What if God's plans for me didn't align with my own? What if He asked me to do something I wasn't ready for?

The irony, of course, is that the things I was clinging to weren't giving me peace. If anything, they were weighing me down. But when you've lived so long in survival mode, holding on to anything—even the things that hurt you—can feel safer than letting go.

One night, everything came to a head. I was sitting alone in my room, staring at the ceiling, and feeling that familiar tension rise in my chest. I had been praying about something specific—a decision I knew I needed to make but had been avoiding for weeks. It wasn't just a practical decision; it was deeply personal. God was asking me to let go of certain friendships that were keeping me tied to my old ways—the sinful patterns and habits I was so desperately trying to leave behind.

These weren't bad people. They were people I cared about, people who had been part of my life for years. But deep down, I knew they weren't helping me grow. They weren't encouraging me to step into the new life God was calling me to. Letting go felt impossible. How could I walk away from people who had been there through so much? How could I explain to them that I was changing, that my priorities were shifting?

As I sat there wrestling with these questions, I finally broke. I said out loud, "God, I don't know how to do this. I don't know how to let go."

In the stillness that followed, I felt Him speak to my heart—not in an audible voice, but in a way that was so clear it couldn't be ignored. He said, "You don't have to do this alone. I'm not asking you to let go without Me—I'm asking you to let go with Me."

Those words sank deep into my soul. For so long, I had been carrying the weight of my decisions on my own shoulders, believing it was up to me to figure everything out. But in that moment, God reminded me that surrender wasn't about facing challenges alone. It wasn't about abandoning my plans and hopes—it was about trusting Him to walk with me through the process.

That night marked a turning point for me. It didn't magically erase my fears or make everything easy, but it did shift my perspective. I began to see surrender not as a loss, but as an act of trust. It wasn't about giving up control for the sake of giving it up—it was about placing my life in the hands of the One who knew me better than I knew myself.

Letting go of resistance didn't happen overnight. It was—and still is—a process. Each day, I had to make the choice to release my grip a little more, to open my heart a little wider, to let God take the lead a little further.

At first, those choices felt small and insignificant. I started by praying differently—not just asking God for things, but asking Him to guide me. I began to pay attention to the quiet nudges He placed on my heart. When He prompted me to reach out to someone I'd hurt, I did it. When He asked me to say no to something that didn't align with His truth, I said no.

Each step felt like a leap of faith. But with every step, I began to see something incredible: God's plans were better than mine. Every time I let go of something I thought I couldn't live without,

God replaced it with something greater—peace, joy, purpose, and a deeper relationship with Him.

Receptivity isn't passive. It's not sitting back and waiting for God to do all the work. It's active—it's choosing to trust Him even when it feels uncomfortable. It's leaning into His promises even when the path ahead isn't clear.

The more I opened my heart to God, the more I began to experience the fullness of His presence. I saw His faithfulness in the small, everyday moments. I felt His provision in ways I couldn't explain. And I realized that surrender wasn't just about letting go of what held me back—it was about receiving what God wanted to give me.

There's a freedom that comes with surrender—a freedom I had never known before. The more I let go of my resistance, the more I felt the weight of my fears and doubts begin to lift. And as that spark of faith grew inside me, I began to see surrender not as a sacrifice, but as an invitation.

An invitation to trust.

An invitation to grow.

An invitation to, step into the life God had been preparing for me all along.

That's the beauty of moving from resistance to receptivity. It's not about losing control; it's about placing your life in the hands of the One who has been guiding you all along. And as you do, you begin to see that His plans are always, always better than your own.

Chapter Seven: When Faith Finds Its Spark

Surrender is where faith begins, but it's not where it ends. When I finally let go of my resistance, I thought I had crossed some sort of finish line. I thought surrender was the destination—an act of giving up control so that God could take the lead. And while that was true, what I didn't realize at the time was that surrender was also a doorway. It opened up space in my heart for something far more profound to grow: faith.

Faith wasn't what I thought it was. I used to see it as something static—an acknowledgment that God exists, that He's real, that He's out there somewhere holding everything together. That kind of faith was neat and contained. It was safe, like an unlit candle sitting on a shelf. But as I began to walk with God, I discovered faith is anything but neat. It's not a candle on a shelf—it's a living fire. It burns, it grows, it moves. And it requires fuel.

Faith starts as a spark. It's small, almost imperceptible at first. It's that faint flicker of hope that whispers, Maybe there's more. It's the quiet voice in your soul that tells you to take a step into the unknown. But like any fire, that spark won't last on its own. It needs to be protected, nurtured, fed. That's what I began to learn in this part of my journey. Faith wasn't just about acknowledging who God is—it was about trusting Him with the unknown and stepping into a life I couldn't yet see.

In the early days, my faith felt fragile. I clung to it like a new mother cradles her baby—careful, uncertain, terrified I might break it. I had experienced God in powerful ways: His grace that lifted my burdens, His conviction that softened my heart, His truth that opened my eyes. But living out that faith was a different story.

I remember wrestling with the question: Is this real? I believed in my head that God was with me, but my heart struggled to trust Him fully. There were moments when doubt crept in, whispering, What if this doesn't work? What if you take a step and fall flat on your face? What if God doesn't come through?

Faith doesn't grow in an instant. It grows step by step, choice by choice. It's not about a single leap into the unknown, but about learning to trust God in the small, ordinary moments of life. For me, it started with things that felt almost insignificant at the time: a whispered prayer late at night when I wasn't even sure God was listening. Opening my Bible for five minutes before bed, even when I didn't feel like it. Asking God for guidance when I wasn't sure what to do.

Each of those small acts of faith felt like a drop in the ocean—too small to matter. But looking back, I can see how God used them to build something far greater than I could have imagined. Each time I trusted Him, even in the smallest of ways, my faith grew a little stronger. Each time I obeyed His nudge, even when it scared me, the spark inside me burned a little brighter.

One of the hardest lessons I had to learn about faith was how to trust God in the waiting. Waiting is uncomfortable. It's frustrating. It feels like wasted time. There were moments when I would pray and hear nothing. Times when I took a step of faith and saw no immediate results.

In those moments, doubt hit the hardest. What's the point? Is God even paying attention? Why isn't anything happening? It felt like I was standing in the middle of an empty field, waiting for rain that never came.

But here's the thing about waiting: it's not wasted time. Waiting is where faith is forged. It's in the silence, the stillness, the uncertainty that faith grows deep roots. It's in the waiting that we learn to trust God not for what He can do, but for who He is.

Hebrews 11:1 says, "Now faith is confidence in what we hope for and assurance about what we do not see."

That verse used to really frustrate me. How could I have confidence in something I couldn't see? How could I trust God when I didn't know what He was doing? But over time, I began to realize faith isn't about certainty—it's about trust. Faith doesn't require me to see the whole picture; it only requires me to trust the One who does.

There's a moment in every faith journey when the spark becomes something more. For me, that moment came when I stopped holding back and fully stepped into what God was asking me to do.

At the time, I was working at a small grocery store in Kingston, Tennessee. The work was simple and unremarkable, but it gave me plenty of time to think. And one day, as I was stocking shelves, I felt a nudge in my spirit—God asking me to share the gospel with one of my coworkers, Steve.

The thought totally terrified me. I wasn't the kind of person who shared my faith openly. I didn't know what to say or how to start. And what if Steve rejected me? What if he laughed in my face? The fear of failing, of looking foolish, was paralyzing.

For days, I wrestled with God. I came up with every excuse I could think of: I'm not ready. Someone else would do a better job. What if I mess this up? After all I have only know God for a short time myself. But no matter how much I resisted; the nudge didn't go away. God wasn't asking me to have all the answers—He was simply asking me to trust Him.

One night, as I lay in bed, I finally surrendered. My prayer wasn't eloquent or polished. It was raw, honest, and full of fear: God, I don't know what I'm doing. I'm scared. But if this is what You're asking me to do, I'll do it.

The next day, I saw Steve in the parking lot after work. My heart was pounding rapidly as I approached him. I didn't have a plan or a rehearsed speech—just a willingness to share my story. I told him how much God had changed my life, how His grace had lifted me out of place of real darkness that I had been living in, and how that same grace was available to him.

Steve listened. He didn't laugh or brush me off. He didn't make any immediate decisions, but he thanked me for sharing my story with him. And you know what? That was enough. God hadn't asked me to guarantee an outcome. He only asked me to take the step.

That moment taught me something I've carried with me ever since: faith isn't passive. It's not something you quietly hold onto while life moves forward. Faith calls you to action. It pushes you to step out of your comfort zone, to trust God with the unknown, to do the thing that scares you, knowing He will meet you there.

But here's the beautiful part: God doesn't expect your faith to be perfect. He doesn't need you to have it all together. He only asks for your willingness.

Each small step of obedience fanned the spark of my faith into a steady flame. It didn't happen all at once. It happened gradually, as I learned to trust God one choice at a time.

Maybe you're feeling that same nudge today. Maybe God is asking you to take a step of faith, and it feels overwhelming. If that's you, I want you to know this: You don't have to have all the answers. You don't have to know exactly what to do. You just have to take the next step and trust that God will take care of the rest.

Faith doesn't mean you never doubt. It means you keep choosing to believe, even when doubts creep in. It means trusting that God is who He says He is, even when the path ahead is unclear.

That's the beauty of faith—it grows not in the absence of uncertainty, but in the middle of it. It starts as a spark, fragile and small, but with each step of trust, it becomes a flame that lights your way and draws you closer to God.

So, what's the step God is asking you to take today? Whatever it is, don't let fear hold you back. Trust Him. Take the step. Because when you do, that spark of faith inside you will grow into something unshakable—a fire that can't be extinguished.

Chapter Eight: Turning Toward the Light, The Act of Repentance

Faith has a way of softening us, of breaking open the hardened places we thought were unchangeable. It moves us forward, leading us closer to God in ways that challenge and transform us. One of the most profound responses to faith—and one of the hardest—is repentance. Not because repentance is complex, but because it requires something deeply vulnerable: honesty.

For a long time, I misunderstood repentance. I thought it was about punishment—something you did because you had failed. To me, repentance felt heavy, like dragging a ball and chain of guilt to God and begging Him to take it off. It seemed rooted in shame, and because of that, I resisted it. But as I grew in my faith, God began to show me a different perspective. He began to show me the beauty of repentance—not as condemnation, but as an invitation.

Repentance is one of the most beautiful gifts God offers us. It's not a doorway to judgment but a pathway to freedom. It's not about hanging your head low in guilt—it's about lifting your eyes to the One who loves you too much to let you stay stuck. At its core, repentance is about turning. It's recognizing the path you're on and choosing to redirect your steps toward the One who knows the way.

But here's the thing I didn't understand for years: repentance isn't about you fixing yourself. It's about surrender. It's about admitting you can't fix yourself and allowing God to step in and do what only He can do.

In its simplest form, repentance means to turn around. It's a change in direction—not just in your actions but in your heart. And yet, that turning doesn't always come easily. For me, it didn't happen all at once. It came in layers, each one peeling back another part of my soul that needed to be surrendered.

There were parts of my life I wasn't ready to let go of. Patterns of thinking I wasn't ready to confront. Habits I didn't want to break. I told myself, It's not a big deal. Nobody's perfect. God knows my heart. But deep down, I knew the truth. I could feel the tension building in my spirit, the quiet whisper of conviction saying, You weren't made for this. There's more for you than this.

That's the thing about sin—it deceives you. It convinces you that you can handle it, that it's not really hurting you. It whispers lies that sound like truth: This is just who you are. You'll never be free from this. You're too far gone for God to care anymore. And for a while, I believed those lies. I carried the weight of my mistakes and my pride, too ashamed to admit how much I needed to let go.

But God doesn't leave us stuck. He doesn't let us drown in the consequences of our own decisions. Instead, He calls to us—gently but persistently—inviting us to turn back to Him. And when we do, everything begins to change.

I remember the night God began to break through my resistance. It wasn't in a dramatic moment of worship or a sermon that shook my soul. It was a quiet, unremarkable night. I was driving home from work, the streetlights casting long shadows on the road ahead. My mind was swirling with thoughts about everything I hadn't done right—relationships I had neglected, words I wished I could take back, choices I knew had pulled me further from God.

As I drove through the silence, I felt a nudge deep in my spirit. It wasn't a voice I could hear, but it was unmistakable: It's time. It's time to stop running. It's time to turn around.

At first, I resisted. I came up with every excuse I could think of: It's not that bad. Other people have done worse. God understands. But no matter how hard I tried to brush it off, the nudge remained. And with it came something unexpected: hope.

You see, repentance isn't about looking back at your mistakes with regret. It's about looking forward to the healing and restoration God is ready to give. That night, as I drove under the quiet glow of the streetlights, I felt God's invitation—not to shame, but to freedom.

When I got home, I sat in the stillness of my room and prayed the most honest prayer I'd ever prayed. It wasn't long or eloquent. It didn't follow any script. It was raw and simple:

God, I'm tired. I'm tired of carrying this weight. I'm tired of running from You. I don't even know where to start, but I know I can't do this on my own. Please help me turn back to You.

In that moment, something shifted. The weight I'd been carrying for so long began to lift—not because I had fixed anything, but because I had finally surrendered. That's the beauty of repentance. It's not about getting everything right. It's about turning to the One who is right and letting Him take the lead.

But repentance isn't just between you and God. Sometimes, it requires action. For me, that meant reaching out to people I had hurt—family members, friends, people I had let down. The thought of apologizing terrified me. What if they didn't forgive me? What if I made things worse? But then God reminded me: Your job isn't to control their response. Your job is to obey.

So, I started making phone calls. I wrote letters. I sat down for awkward, humbling conversations. Some people forgave me instantly. Others needed time. But with each act of obedience, I felt God working—not just in their hearts, but in mine.

Repentance isn't just about seeking forgiveness—it's about restoration. It's about letting God heal the broken parts of your life, one step at a time.

One of the most powerful truths I've learned about repentance is this: God isn't waiting to punish you. He's waiting to welcome you back.

1 John 1:9 says, "If we confess our sins, He is faithful and just and will forgive us our sins and purify us from all unrighteousness."

That's the promise of repentance. When we turn to God, He doesn't meet us with condemnation. He meets us with open arms.

For years, I thought repentance was about fixing myself so I could be good enough for God. But the truth is, repentance isn't about fixing anything—it's about surrendering everything. It's about bringing your brokenness to God and allowing Him to do the work of transformation.

Repentance isn't a one-time event. It's not something you do once and move past. It's a daily decision to turn back to God, again and again. Not because He's waiting to catch you messing up, but because our hearts so easily wander.

Sometimes, repentance is big and obvious—a moment of breaking free from a destructive habit or mindset. Other times, it's quieter—a choice to let go of bitterness, to forgive someone who hurt you, to pause in the middle of a busy day and realign your heart with God.

Each act of repentance, no matter how small, is a step closer to the light.

Maybe today, you're feeling the weight of something—a mistake, a habit, a relationship that needs healing. Maybe you're hearing that quiet nudge in your heart, calling you to turn back. If that's where you are, I want you to know this: God isn't angry with you. He's not waiting to punish or shame you. He's waiting to welcome you home.

Repentance is a gift. It's God's invitation to step out of the shadows and into His light. It's about trusting Him to take the broken pieces of your life and make something beautiful.

So, take a moment to reflect. What are you holding onto that you need to let go of? Where is God calling you to turn back to Him?

Then take that first step. It doesn't have to be perfect. It doesn't have to be big. Just turn toward Him. Because when you do, you'll find that He's already there, waiting to meet you with grace, love, and open arms.

And in His light, you'll finally find freedom.

Chapter Nine : A New Birth of Hope

Hope is a fragile thing. At least, that's how it had always felt to me. It was something I had clung to in fleeting moments, something that flared up only to flicker out when life became too heavy to bear. For most of my life, hope had seemed like a mirage—something I wanted to believe in but couldn't hold onto for long. It wasn't that I didn't want hope; I just didn't trust it. How could I, when the weight of my choices and circumstances had crushed it so many times before?

But as I continued my journey with God—learning to trust Him, surrender to Him, and turn toward Him in repentance—something began to shift. Hope wasn't just an abstract concept anymore. It was becoming real, tangible, alive. For the first time, I felt it stirring within me, not as a fleeting feeling, but as a steady presence—a light growing stronger with every step I took toward God.

This hope wasn't based on circumstances. It wasn't rooted in the fragile promises of the world or in my own ability to keep my life together. It was rooted in something—or rather, Someone—unchanging. It was hope born from the knowledge that God was with me, that He was working in my life, and that He wasn't finished with me yet.

Hope doesn't arrive all at once. It doesn't burst into your life like fireworks. It starts small, almost imperceptible, like the first hint of dawn after a long, dark night. You don't even realize it's there at first. But as it grows, it begins to change the way you see everything.

For me, the birth of hope came in stages. It started with the smallest of realizations: that God wasn't distant. He wasn't sitting on some faraway throne, waiting for me to get my act together. He was close—closer than I had ever imagined. He was walking with me, guiding me, and working in ways I couldn't yet see.

That realization alone began to change my perspective. Life didn't feel as overwhelming as it once had. The struggles I was facing—the ones that had felt so suffocating—started to feel smaller in the light of God's presence. It wasn't that my circumstances had changed overnight. The challenges were still there. But hope gave me the strength to face them.

Hope, I began to realize, isn't the absence of struggle. It's the certainty that struggle doesn't get the final word.

There was a verse I stumbled upon during this time that became like an anchor for me:

"May the God of hope fill you with all joy and peace as you trust in Him, so that you may overflow with hope by the power of the Holy Spirit" (Romans 15:13).

That word—overflow—stuck with me. Hope wasn't just meant to be a flicker of light in the darkness. It was meant to overflow, to pour out of me and into every corner of my life. But how could that happen? How could I move from barely holding onto hope to living a life overflowing with it?

The answer was right there in the verse: as you trust in Him.

Hope and trust are inseparable. The more I trusted God, the more hope grew in my heart. Trusting God didn't mean I suddenly had all the answers or that life became easy. It meant choosing to believe that He was who He said He was—that He was good, faithful, and loving, even when I couldn't see the full picture.

One of the most profound lessons I learned during this season was that hope isn't passive. It's not something you wait for—it's something you step into. Hope requires action. It requires a willingness to move forward, even when you're not sure where the path will lead.

For me, that meant taking small, practical steps to live out the hope that was taking root in my heart. It meant choosing to show up each day with a heart open to what God wanted to do. It meant stepping out of my comfort zone and saying yes to opportunities that scared me. It meant looking for ways to serve others, even when I felt like I didn't have much to give.

One of those opportunities came in the form of a small Bible study group at my aunt's church. At first, I was hesitant to join. I still felt like a work in progress—too messy, too unpolished to sit in a circle and talk about faith with other people. But something in me knew this was the next step God was asking me to take.

So, I showed up. And week after week, as I listened to others share their struggles and their victories, I began to see how hope was working in their lives, too. It wasn't loud or flashy. It was quiet, steady, unshakable. Their stories reminded me that hope isn't something you have to manufacture on your own. It's a gift that grows as you walk with God and surround yourself with people who are walking with Him, too.

Another lesson God taught me about hope is that it requires patience. We live in a world that demands instant results, but hope doesn't work that way. It grows over time, like a seed planted in the ground. You don't see the fruit right away, but that doesn't mean nothing is happening.

There were days when I felt like I wasn't making any progress, like I was stuck in the same struggles I'd been facing for years. But hope reminded me that God's timing is different from mine. He wasn't just interested in changing my circumstances—He was interested in changing my heart.

Waiting isn't easy, but hope gives you the strength to wait well. It reminds you that God is always at work, even in the waiting. And it fills you with the confidence that His plans for you are good, even when you can't see how everything will come together.

One of the most beautiful things about hope is that it doesn't just change you—it changes the way you see the world. As hope grew in my heart, I started to notice things I had overlooked before. I saw beauty in the small, ordinary moments of life—a kind word from a stranger, the laughter of a child, the way the sunlight filtered through the trees on a quiet afternoon.

I began to see the people around me differently, too. I saw their struggles, their pain, their need for the same hope that was transforming me. And I realized that hope wasn't just something for me to hold onto—it was something to share.

Hope isn't meant to be kept to yourself. It's meant to be a light that shines into the darkness, a reminder to others that they're not alone.

I started to look for ways to share the hope I had found, even in small ways. A kind word, a listening ear, a prayer offered in the quiet of my heart. It wasn't about preaching or trying to "fix" anyone. It was about being present, about letting the hope within me overflow into the lives of those around me.

One of the most powerful moments came when I reconnected with an old friend from Michigan who was going through a difficult time. On one of our phone calls, I shared a bit of my journey—not in a way that felt rehearsed or forced, but simply and honestly. I told her about how God had met me in my lowest moments, how He had lifted the weight I'd been carrying, and how He was slowly but surely changing my life.

I didn't know how she would respond, but that wasn't the point. The point was to share the hope I had been given and trust God to do the rest.

Hope isn't always loud or dramatic. Sometimes it's as simple as showing up, as quiet as a prayer whispered in the stillness of the night. But even in its quietest moments, hope is powerful. It's the thing that keeps you moving forward when everything in you wants to give up. It's the light that guides you when the path ahead feels uncertain.

As I look back on this season of my life, I can see how God used hope to transform me—not just my circumstances, but my heart. Hope didn't erase the struggles I faced, but it gave me the strength to face them. It didn't guarantee an easy road, but it reminded me that I wasn't walking that road alone.

Maybe you're in a place right now where hope feels far away. Maybe life has worn you down, and you're not sure if you can believe things will ever get better. If that's where you are, I want you to know this: Hope is closer than you think. It's not something you have to earn or create on your own. It's a gift from God, and He's ready to pour it into your heart if you'll let Him.

Take that first step toward Him. Open your heart to the possibility that He's not finished with you yet. Because He isn't.

Hope isn't fragile. It's a fire that burns steadily, even in the darkest night. And when you let it take root in your heart, it has the power to change everything.

THE JOURNEY

Chapter Ten: Freedom to Choose, Freedom to Live

Freedom. It's a word that's held power over humanity for as long as we've existed. Wars have been fought for it, lives sacrificed in its name, and entire movements built on its promise. But what is freedom, really? Is it the absence of restrictions? The ability to live life on your own terms? For most of my life, I thought freedom meant exactly that—living however I wanted, without anyone telling me what to do.

But the freedom I chased wasn't freedom at all. It was a mirage, a lie wrapped in shiny packaging, promising happiness and fulfillment but delivering the opposite. Instead of feeling free, I felt trapped—trapped by my choices, my desires, and my inability to find peace.

True freedom, I've come to realize, isn't about doing whatever you want. It's about being free from the things that hold you captive. It's about shedding the chains of fear, shame, and self-reliance and stepping into the life God created you to live. And most importantly, it's about learning that freedom begins with a choice—the choice to trust God and let Him lead you.

From the beginning of creation, God gave humanity the freedom to choose. It's one of the most profound gifts He's ever given us. He didn't create us to be robots or puppets, forced to follow Him without question. Instead, He gave us the ability to decide for ourselves—to choose whether we would walk in His ways or go our own way.

That gift of free will is a reflection of His love. Love isn't real unless it's chosen, and God desires a relationship with us that's built on love, not coercion. But with that freedom comes responsibility. Our choices matter. They shape the direction of our lives and the condition of our hearts.

For years, I didn't understand the weight of my choices. I thought freedom meant doing whatever made me happy in the moment. If it felt good, if it didn't seem to hurt anyone else, I thought it was fine. But what I didn't realize was that every decision I made was shaping me—slowly, subtly, but surely.

The world tells us that freedom is about following our hearts, pursuing our dreams, and living without restrictions. But what the world doesn't tell us is that our hearts can deceive us, our dreams can lead us astray, and the pursuit of self can leave us empty. True freedom isn't found in doing whatever you want—it's found in becoming who you were created to be.

The choices I made in my past led me down paths that promised freedom but left me feeling more enslaved than ever. I chased approval, thinking it would make me feel valued. I pursued comfort, thinking it would give me peace. I clung to control, thinking it would make me feel secure. But none of it worked.

The more I tried to free myself, the more trapped I became. The approval I sought never lasted. The comfort I chased only numbed me temporarily. And the control I clung to was an illusion—I couldn't control my circumstances, and I certainly couldn't control the deep ache in my heart that told me something was missing.

What I didn't understand at the time was that I wasn't just chasing freedom—I was chasing fulfillment. And the two are deeply connected. True fulfillment can only be found in true freedom. But true freedom doesn't come from within us. It comes from God.

One of the most beautiful truths I've learned about freedom is this: it's not something you have to earn. You don't have to work for it, strive for it, or prove yourself worthy of it. Freedom is a gift—a gift that was made possible through Jesus.

When Jesus died on the cross, He didn't just take the punishment for our sins. He broke the power of sin over our lives. He made a way for us to be free—free from guilt, free from shame, free from the lies that tell us we're not enough.

But here's the thing: freedom is a gift that requires a response. God doesn't force it on us. He offers it to us, but we have to choose to receive it. And receiving that freedom often requires us to let go of the very things we've been holding onto—things we thought would bring us freedom but have only held us back.

For me, that process of letting go was anything but easy. I had spent years clinging to control, thinking I could figure out life on my own. Surrender felt like failure, like admitting I wasn't strong enough or capable enough to handle things on my own. But what I've come to understand is that surrender isn't weakness—it's strength. It's the strength to admit that you can't do it on your own and to trust that God can.

When I finally surrendered my need for control, something incredible happened. The chains I had been carrying—the fear, the shame, the relentless need to prove myself—began to fall away. I didn't feel lighter because my circumstances had changed. I felt lighter because I wasn't carrying the weight alone anymore.

God's freedom isn't just about setting us free from something—it's about setting us free for something. It's about stepping into the purpose He has for us, the life He created us to live.

One of the first times I truly experienced the freedom to live came wrapped in an opportunity I didn't think I was ready for. It started when Pastor Tim, the pastor at the church of one of my closest friends Wes & Kelly, approached me with a challenge that stopped me in my tracks. He asked me to lead a Bible study for a small group. On paper, it seemed simple enough—just gather a group, open the Bible, and guide a discussion. But for me, it felt anything but simple. Deep down, I felt waves of doubt and fear rising up.

At the time, I was still relatively new to understanding meant to walk with God. I was still learning, still stumbling, trying to grasp the depth of His grace and purpose for my life. The idea of standing in front of a group of people and leading them through Scripture made me feel like an imposter. I wasn't a pastor. I wasn't a theologian. I wasn't the kind of person who had memorized every verse or understood every nuance of the Bible. All I could see were the gaps in my knowledge, the cracks in my confidence, and the nagging feeling that someone else—anyone else—would be better suited for the task.

"What if I don't know enough?" I thought. "What if someone asks me a question I can't answer? What if I completely mess it up?" The questions swirled in my mind, feeding my insecurity with every passing moment. To me, the people who led Bible studies were confident, polished, and spiritually mature. They were the kind of people who could quote Scripture effortlessly, people who seemed to have their spiritual lives figured out. And I, by comparison, felt painfully inadequate.

When I shared my concerns with Pastor Tim, hoping he might let me off the hook, he didn't waver for a second. Instead, he smiled with the quiet confidence of someone who had been in my shoes before. "God doesn't call the equipped," he said gently. "He equips the called."

Those words landed in my heart like a lifeline. They were simple, yet filled with truth. God wasn't asking me to be perfect. He wasn't looking for someone with all the answers. He was looking for someone willing to say yes. And yet, even with those words of encouragement ringing in my ears, I wrestled with hesitation. The idea of saying yes felt daunting, as though I were stepping into something far bigger than I was prepared for.

For several days, I went back and forth in my mind. I thought about declining. I considered telling Wes or Pastor Tim that I just wasn't ready. "There's no shame in admitting you're not cut out for this," I told myself. But beneath my excuses, something deeper stirred—a quiet, persistent nudge that I couldn't ignore. Maybe this wasn't about being "ready." Maybe this was about trusting God to work through me, despite my fears, doubts, and shortcomings.

Hesitantly, I said yes.

As soon as I committed, the nerves kicked in. The weeks leading up to the study were filled with preparation—and prayer. I spent hours diving into Scripture, taking notes, and praying for wisdom. I pored over the passages we'd be discussing, scribbling thoughts in the margins of my Bible and writing questions I hoped would spark meaningful conversations. But no matter how much I prepared; I couldn't shake the nagging doubt: "What if I'm not enough?"

The night before the first study, I couldn't sleep. I lay awake, staring at the ceiling, replaying every worst-case scenario in my mind. But in the stillness of that night, as I whispered one last nervous prayer, I felt something stir in my heart. It wasn't loud or dramatic, but it was steady and sure: "You don't have to do this alone. I'll give you what you need."

The night of the study, I arrived early, hoping to steady my nerves before the group arrived. One by one, people began trickling into the room, flipping through their Bibles and greeting each other with warm smiles. I tried to focus on their kindness instead of the fear tightening in my chest. These weren't strangers—they were people, just like me, who were seeking to know God more deeply. They weren't expecting perfection. They were simply there to learn, to share, and to grow together.

When it was finally time to begin, I stood in front of the group with my heart pounding. My hands felt clammy, and for a moment, I questioned whether I could actually do this. But as I looked around the room, something unexpected happened. I felt a quiet peace settle over me. These people weren't here to judge me—they were here to meet with God. And in that moment, I realized it wasn't about me at all. It was about Him.

I opened with a prayer, my voice trembling slightly, but as I spoke, I felt the words flow more freely. When I started walking the group through the passage, something incredible happened. The verses I had spent so much time studying seemed to come alive. The words I had been afraid of forgetting came to me with clarity and confidence—not because I had suddenly become an expert, but because I was relying on God to guide me.

The more I spoke, the more I felt His presence in the room. When someone asked a question, I didn't panic. Instead, I leaned on the Holy Spirit, trusting Him to give me the words or the humility to admit when I didn't have an answer. When I shared my reflections, I felt a sense of authenticity I hadn't expected. And as others began to share their own thoughts and stories, I realized that leading wasn't about being the smartest person in the room—it was about creating a space where God could move.

By the end of the night, I was in awe—not of myself, but of what God had done. He had taken my fear, my doubt, and my insecurity and transformed them into opportunities to reveal His strength. He reminded me that it wasn't about my ability—it was about His faithfulness.

That experience taught me something I'll carry with me for the rest of my life: God's freedom doesn't just release you from your past—it empowers you for your future. True freedom isn't about living a life free from challenges—it's about living a life free to say yes to God, free to step into the unknown, and free to trust Him with the outcome.

Before that night, I thought of freedom as something passive—a state of being that came after you let go of fear or shame. But what I discovered is that true freedom is active. It calls you to take risks, to step outside your comfort zone, and to trust that God will meet you there.

Looking back, I'm deeply and profoundly grateful to Pastor Tim for encouraging me to take that step—a step I would have never taken on my own. Pastor Tim has been, and continues to be, a man of God whom I deeply love and respect. His wisdom, humility, and encouragement reflect a faith that inspires everyone around him, including me. When I doubted myself, when I questioned my abilities and thought someone else would be better suited, Pastor Tim saw something I couldn't see in myself. He saw potential—not for my own glory, but for God's. And in his gentle but firm encouragement, he reminded me of a truth I desperately needed to hear: God doesn't call the equipped; He equips the called.

At the time, I thought leading that Bible study would be an opportunity to serve others, to step out of my comfort zone and contribute something meaningful. What I didn't expect was for it to be a pivotal moment in my own spiritual journey. That experience taught me lessons I'll carry with me for the rest of my life. And as much as I'm thankful for Pastor Tim's encouragement, I'm even more grateful to God for showing me, firsthand, what becomes possible when we surrender our fears, doubts, and limitations to Him.

That first Bible study wasn't just a learning experience for the group—it was a profound lesson for me. In many ways, it was less about teaching Scripture and more about God using the experience to transform me. It challenged me to confront my insecurities, lean into God's strength, and trust that He could work through me despite my doubts. I walked into that experience expecting to lead others. What I didn't realize was how much God was going to use that time to lead me—to stretch me, teach me, and deepen my faith in ways I couldn't have imagined.

What I learned during those weeks is something that continues to shape the way I live, serve, and follow God today: the person who learns the most from any study is almost always the teacher.

At first, that thought seemed counterintuitive. Shouldn't the teacher—the one tasked with guiding and instructing others—already know everything there is to know about the subject? But teaching is different. It's not about presenting yourself as an expert. It's about showing up with humility, willing to wrestle with the material, ask the hard questions, and open yourself to what God wants to reveal. Leading that study pushed me deeper into Scripture than I had ever gone before. I spent hours praying, reflecting, and seeking God's guidance—not just so I could teach others, but because I realized how much I still needed to learn.

I went into it thinking my role was to teach others about God's truth. What I didn't expect was how much God would use that experience to teach me. He showed me that leadership in His kingdom isn't about expertise, eloquence, or having it all figured out. It's about humility. It's about being vulnerable enough to admit you don't have all the answers. And most importantly, it's about having a willing heart—a heart that says, "Here I am, Lord. Use me."

During those weeks of preparation and prayer, I began to understand a truth I had never fully grasped before: God doesn't need perfection to do His work. He doesn't need polished performances or flawless presentations. He doesn't need someone who has every answer memorized or never makes a mistake. What He needs—what He desires—is a heart that's willing to say yes. A heart that says, "I don't have it all together, but I trust You, God, to work through me anyway."

That realization changed everything for me. It took the pressure off. It wasn't about me being good enough—it was about God being more than enough. It wasn't about my ability—it was about His faithfulness. And as I stepped into that truth, I found a freedom I had never known before.

That doesn't mean the Bible study was perfect. There were moments when I stumbled over my words. Moments when I didn't know how to answer a question. Moments when I felt the weight of my inexperience pressing down on me. But through it all, God was faithful. He took my small, hesitant "yes," and He used it in ways I could never have orchestrated on my own. He worked through my fears, my doubts, and even my mistakes to plant seeds—not just in the hearts of the group members, but in my own heart as well.

One of the most humbling moments came as I listened to the group share their thoughts, ask questions, and wrestle with the Scriptures. I realized how much God was working in real time—not just through me, but in me. Their insights, their prayers, and the ways they connected God's Word to their own lives were reminders that I was just one part of what God was doing. The pressure wasn't on me to perform or to have all the answers. My job was simply to create space for God to move—and He did.

He moved in ways I couldn't have anticipated, in ways that humbled me and reminded me of His sovereignty. He reminded me that when we step out in faith, even when we feel unprepared, He meets us there. He doesn't just fill in the gaps—He goes far beyond anything we could ask or imagine.

Perhaps the most surprising lesson I learned from that Bible study was this: ministry is as much about the teacher's growth as it is about the students. Leading that group forced me to confront areas of my own faith that needed strengthening. It deepened my relationship with God, gave me a renewed hunger for His Word, and showed me just how much I still have to learn. And it reminded me that we are all students in the school of grace, constantly learning, growing, and being transformed by God's love.

I've come to believe that God uses these moments of stretching—moments when we feel inadequate or unprepared—not to expose our weaknesses, but to reveal His strength. When I think back to that Bible study, I don't see it as a moment where I proved myself as a leader. I see it as a moment where God proved His faithfulness. He took my nervous, trembling "yes" and turned it into something beautiful. He reminded me that His power is made perfect in our weakness and that all He asks of us is to trust Him enough to take the next step.

Looking back now, I see that Bible study as a turning point in my faith. It was the moment I stopped waiting to feel "ready" and started saying yes to God, even when I felt unsure. It was the moment I realized that obedience doesn't require certainty—it requires trust. And it was the moment I began to see myself not as someone defined by my limitations, but as someone defined by God's limitless grace.

So, if you're reading this and you feel unqualified, if you feel like you don't have what it takes to step into what God is calling you to do, I want to share the same encouragement Pastor Tim gave me: God doesn't call the equipped—He equips the called. You don't have to have all the answers. You don't have to have it all together. You just have to be willing to say yes.

God doesn't need perfection to do His work. He simply needs a willing heart. And when you offer Him that—when you take the step of faith and trust Him to lead you—you'll discover that He's been preparing you all along. You'll find that His strength is more than enough, that His grace is sufficient, and that His plans for you are greater than anything you could have imagined.

That Bible study wasn't just a lesson for the group—it was a lesson for me. It was a reminder that God's power is not limited by our insecurities. It was an invitation to step into the freedom of living a life surrendered to Him. And it was the beginning of a journey I'm still on—a journey of trusting God, one step at a time, and watching Him work in ways I never thought possible.

Freedom isn't just about us—it's about others, too. As I stepped into the freedom God was offering me, I began to see how that freedom could overflow into the lives of those around me. The more I experienced God's love and grace, the more I wanted to share it with others.

True freedom is relational. It's not about living for yourself—it's about living in community with others, showing them the same love and grace that God has shown you.

Maybe you're reading this and thinking, "That kind of freedom sounds great, but it's not for me. You don't know what I've done. You don't know the mistakes I've made."

If that's where you are, I want you to know this: God's freedom isn't reserved for the perfect. It's not just for the people who have it all together. It's for you, right where you are.

God's freedom is a gift—and like any gift, it's not something you can earn. It's something you simply receive.

So, if you're feeling weighed down today—by fear, by shame, by the need to control—know that you don't have to carry that weight any longer. God is offering you freedom. All you have to do is say yes.

And when you do, you'll discover that His freedom isn't just about letting go of the past. It's about stepping into the life you were created to live—a life full of purpose, joy, and connection.

This is the freedom to choose. This is the freedom to live. And it's yours for the taking.

This is the promise of hope: no matter where you've been or what you've done, God is with you. He's working in your life. And He's leading you toward something beautiful. So, take heart. Hold onto hope. And trust that the One who began a good work in you will be faithful to complete it.

THE JOURNEY

Chapter Eleven: Entering the Family of God

Belonging. It's one of those words that carries weight, a word that can stir up longing or even pain. For much of my life, I thought belonging came from the approval of others—being liked, accepted, or included. I worked hard to earn that sense of connection, even if it meant wearing a mask or playing a role that wasn't fully me. If I could just be enough—smart enough, good enough, successful enough—then maybe I would feel that I belonged.

But the more I chased it, the more I realized how fragile and fleeting that kind of belonging is. It didn't matter how many friends I had or how many people smiled when I walked into a room; there was still a quiet ache deep inside me. It wasn't loneliness in the obvious sense. I wasn't isolated. I wasn't disconnected from others entirely. Yet I felt like a stranger, even to myself.

Then God stepped in.

The last few chapters of my life had been about surrender—surrendering my pride, my control, my resistance, and my misconceptions about faith. I had come to the altar and felt grace lift a weight I didn't know I was carrying. I had begun to trust in God's conviction and truth, choosing to turn from the paths that led me away from Him and, instead, toward His light. My faith had sparked to life like a fragile flame and grown stronger with each step of obedience—each small "yes" to God.

But faith, I was learning, wasn't just about believing. It was about belonging. And belonging to God meant belonging to His family.

That idea felt foreign at first. God's grace had felt deeply personal—something between Him and me. My moments of prayer, surrender, and conviction were private. I saw them as part of my own journey, an individual relationship I was building with God. I didn't think I needed anyone else to walk that road with me. Honestly, I wasn't even sure I wanted to let anyone in. After all, relationships are messy. People let you down. Vulnerability opens the door for rejection. And I'd spent so much of my life protecting myself from those very things.

But as I look back now, I can see that God, in His wisdom, was gently leading me into something far greater. Faith, while personal, was never meant to be private. From the very beginning, God's plan for His people has been relational. He created us not only for connection with Him but for connection with one another.

And as He often does, God used the circumstances of my life to teach me this truth.

When my wife, Joy, and I decided to move our family from the suburbs of Detroit to a small country village, we had no idea what God was preparing for us. At the time, we were simply looking for a fresh start. Life in the city had taken its toll—its constant noise, the unrelenting pace, and the unspoken pressure to keep up. We wanted something different for our two young children, Shalyn and

Jared. A quieter life. More space to grow. A chance to breathe and refocus on what mattered most.

So, we packed up our lives and moved, hopeful but unsure of what we would find.

At first, the change felt disorienting. The slower pace of the countryside was both refreshing and unnerving. I wasn't used to quiet roads and neighbors who waved as they passed. Life here felt simpler, but it also felt unfamiliar. For all the peace we had hoped to find, there was still a lingering sense of being outsiders, of not yet belonging.

That's when we found the church.

Or maybe, I should say, the church found us.

It started with an invitation from a neighbor. "You should come visit," they said casually one afternoon, as if it were the most natural thing in the world. Joy and I talked about it that evening, both of us hesitant but curious. I had grown up around church, but my past experiences left me unsure. Would we be welcomed, or would we feel out of place? Would this be another environment where we had to pretend to have it all together?

Still, something stirred in us—a quiet nudge, a pull we couldn't ignore. So that Sunday, we loaded the kids into the car and went.

Walking through those church doors for the first time, I didn't know what to expect. But what we found was something I'll never forget. It wasn't just the warm smiles or the friendly handshakes—though those were certainly there. It was something deeper. It was as if we had stepped into a space where grace was tangible, where love wasn't just spoken about but lived out.

The pastor Dale and his wife Deloris were among the first to greet us. They didn't treat us like strangers or visitors. They treated us like family. They asked questions, listened to our story, and made us feel seen. I remember thinking, This is different. There was no pretense here, no pressure to impress anyone or earn our place. It felt… safe.

We kept coming back, week after week. At first, we sat quietly in the pews, just taking it all in. But as the weeks turned into months, something began to shift. We weren't just attending church; we were becoming part of the family.

We joined a small group and found ourselves sitting around dinner tables with other families, sharing meals and stories. We went on group camping trips where laughter echoed late into the night and our kids' made friends of their own. We experienced the beauty of a community that showed up for one another—not just on Sundays, but in the everyday messiness of life.

Slowly, I began to let my guard down. I started to see that this wasn't just a group of people gathering out of obligation. This was a family—God's family—brought together by a grace that bound us to one another.

It was through this community that I began to understand the truth of Ephesians 1:5:

"God decided in advance to adopt us into his own family by bringing us to himself through Jesus Christ. This is what he wanted to do, and it gave him great pleasure."

Adoption. That word held so much weight. It meant that God didn't just accept me—He chose me. I wasn't a guest in His house or an outsider looking in. I was His child. Fully loved. Fully known. Fully welcomed. And if God had adopted me, then He had adopted others too. We were brothers and sisters—not because of anything we had done, but because of what Jesus had done for us.

For the first time, I understood that belonging to God meant belonging to His people. His family.

The Bible describes this family as the body of Christ.

In 1 Corinthians 12:27, Paul writes: "All of you together are Christ's body, and each of you is a part of it."

That means each of us has a role to play. None of us are unnecessary. None of us are alone. We are connected, interwoven, and dependent on one another.

I used to think that belonging was about fitting in, about finding people who liked me for who I appeared to be. But God's family is different. Belonging here isn't about perfection; it's about grace. It's about showing up, being real, and loving one another in the way that God first loved us.

Of course, it's not always easy. Just like any family, there are misunderstandings, disagreements, and frustrations. But what sets God's family apart is the way we keep choosing grace. The way we forgive, reconcile, and show up for one another—again and again.

If you've ever felt like you don't belong, I want you to know this: there is a place for you in God's family. You don't have to earn it. You don't have to prove yourself worthy of it. You are welcome because Jesus made the way for you.

For Joy and me, stepping into God's family changed everything. It showed us that we weren't alone. It reminded us that faith isn't something we walk out in isolation; it's something we live out together. Through the love of God's people, I began to understand His love more deeply.

So, wherever you are today—whether you're searching for belonging or afraid to trust again—I want to encourage you: take a step. Say yes to the invitation. Let yourself be known.

Because when you enter the family of God, you're not just finding a community—you're coming home.

Welcome to the family. You belong here.

THE JOURNEY

Chapter Twelve: Baptism, A Public Declaration of Faith

There's something about water that speaks to the soul. It refreshes, cleanses, and sustains life. It can be calm and peaceful, or fierce and powerful, capable of reshaping entire landscapes. In Scripture, water is woven throughout God's story, marking moments of transformation, rescue, and renewal. Water is the Red Sea parting to deliver God's people from slavery. It's the Samaritan woman meeting Jesus at the well and finding living water that satisfies her deepest spiritual thirst. It's Jesus calming the raging storm with a simple command. Water is never just water in God's hands—it is a symbol of His power to renew, redeem, and make all things new.

So it makes perfect sense that water plays a central role in one of the most profound and significant steps of faith: baptism.

As a child, I didn't fully understand what baptism was all about. I had seen it happen in church—the pastor gently lowering people into a pool or river, the crowd clapping as the newly baptized person emerged, dripping and smiling. It looked meaningful, but I thought of it as little more than a religious tradition. Something Christians did because they were supposed to. I didn't grasp the weight of it—the depth of what it symbolized or why it mattered so much.

But as I grew in my faith, as God slowly tore down my pride, my doubts, and my resistance, I started to see baptism in a whole new light. I came to understand that baptism wasn't just a ritual or a symbolic gesture—it was a declaration. It was obedience. It was a powerful public testimony of the inward transformation God had already begun.

In Romans 6:4, the apostle Paul paints a beautiful picture of what baptism represents:

"We were therefore buried with Him through baptism into death in order that, just as Christ was raised from the dead through the glory of the Father, we too may live a new life."

When we go under the water, it symbolizes the death of our old selves—our sin, our shame, and our brokenness being buried once and for all. And when we rise from the water, it's a vivid picture of the new life we have in Christ—clean, forgiven, and made whole. Baptism doesn't save us; only faith in Jesus does that. But baptism is a bold outward expression of that faith. It's a declaration that we belong to Jesus and have been made new by His grace.

As I reflected on baptism, one truth struck me deeply: Jesus Himself was baptized. Let that sink in. The Son of God, perfect and without sin, stepped into the waters of baptism.

In Matthew 3:13-17, we read the account:

"Then Jesus came from Galilee to the Jordan to be baptized by John. But John tried to deter him, saying, 'I need to be baptized by you, and do you come to me?' Jesus replied, 'Let it be so now; it is proper for us to do this to fulfill all righteousness.' Then John consented.

As soon as Jesus was baptized, he went up out of the water. At that moment heaven was opened, and he saw the Spirit of God descending like a dove and alighting on him. And a voice from heaven said, 'This is my Son, whom I love; with him I am well pleased.'"

Jesus didn't need baptism for repentance—He had no sin to repent of. But He chose baptism to set an example for us, to demonstrate His obedience to the Father, and to mark the beginning of His public ministry. If baptism mattered to Jesus, it should matter to us too.

For me, only a few weeks had passed since that life-altering Sunday morning when God's love and grace broke through every wall I had built. It was the day everything changed—the day I truly surrendered my heart to Him. In that moment, it was as if scales had fallen from my eyes, and I could finally see the truth: I was loved, forgiven, and free.

But even in the joy of that transformation, I could sense God gently calling me to more. There was another step of faith He was asking me to take—baptism.

At first, I hesitated. I knew baptism wasn't what saved me; my salvation was secure in Jesus alone. But this wasn't about salvation. It was about obedience. It was about aligning my outward life with the inward work God had already done. It was about declaring, not just to myself but to everyone watching, "I belong to Christ."

The decision didn't come quickly or lightly. I spent days—weeks, really—praying about it. I read through Scripture, seeking clarity and reassurance. I revisited Paul's words in Romans and reflected on the example of Jesus. The more I prayed, the more it became clear: this was the next step God was calling me to take.

I knew that my baptism couldn't be just a momentary act. It couldn't be a ritual or a box to check off. It needed to be a turning point, a milestone I could look back on as a declaration of my commitment to follow Jesus, no matter where He led.

The day of my baptism is etched into my memory. It was a warm, sunny afternoon, the kind of day that feels like a blessing in itself. Our church had chosen a quiet river outside of town for the baptism service, and as I stood at the water's edge, I was surrounded by people who had been part of my journey—my family, my friends, and my church community.

As I prepared to step into the water, I felt a mix of emotions swirling inside me. Nervousness. Excitement. Humility. Peace. Doubts tried to creep in—What if I stumble? What if people think this is just for show?—but I reminded myself that this moment wasn't about me. It was about Jesus.

The water was cool and calm as I waded in, the pastor standing beside me, offering quiet encouragement. In those few steps, I thought about everything God had done in my life—how He had pursued me, broken down my pride, and filled the empty places in my heart with His love.

When the pastor asked, "Have you placed your trust in Jesus as your Lord and Savior?" I responded with a firm, "Yes."

And as he gently lowered me into the water, it felt as though time itself stood still. The world fell silent, and in that moment, I felt the weight of my past—my fears, my failures, my shame—being buried.

When I rose up from the water, the sunlight hit my face, and I felt an overwhelming sense of joy and freedom. It wasn't about the water itself—there was nothing magical about it. But that act of obedience, of surrender, was powerful. It was a physical picture of the spiritual reality God had brought about in my life: the old had gone, and the new had come.

That's the heart of baptism. It's not about waiting until you feel worthy or ready—it's about responding to God's call and declaring, "I have been made new."

If you've trusted Jesus but haven't yet taken the step of baptism, I want to encourage you: don't wait. Don't let fear or doubt hold you back. Baptism isn't about having everything figured out; it's about being willing. It's about saying, "I belong to Christ."

Because when you step into that water, you're not just getting wet. You're stepping into a story of redemption and grace—a story that began with Jesus and continues with you.

"Therefore, if anyone is in Christ, the new creation has come: The old has gone, the new is here!" (2 Corinthians 5:17,)

It's a story worth celebrating. It's a story worth sharing. And it all begins with a simple, courageous step of faith.

THE JOURNEY

Chapter Thirteen: Growth After Grace, Nurturing the New Life

Baptism is a moment that leaves a mark on your heart. It's a public declaration of faith, a celebration of God's redeeming grace, and a step of obedience that signals the beginning of something new. I vividly remember rising from the water on the day of my baptism, the sunlight streaming down, and the overwhelming sense of joy and peace that flooded my soul. It was a moment of clarity, a tangible reminder that I belonged to Christ.

But as significant as that moment was, it wasn't the conclusion of my journey—it was the beginning. What I didn't fully understand at the time was that baptism, while powerful and beautiful, wasn't a finish line. It was a starting point. The Christian life doesn't stop with the decision to follow Jesus; it begins there. And while grace changes us in an instant, growth takes time.

In those first few weeks after my baptism, I experienced a sort of spiritual high—joy, excitement, and a new awareness of God's presence in my life. But it wasn't long before reality set in. I remember asking myself questions I hadn't anticipated: Why am I still struggling with old habits and thoughts? Why doesn't everything feel as easy as I thought it would? Am I failing somehow?

It's a tension that so many believers experience but don't always talk about. We're filled with gratitude for what God has done in our lives, but we're also painfully aware of how far we still have to go. In those moments, it's easy to feel discouraged, as though we're not doing enough or aren't "good enough" Christians.

But here's the truth I had to learn—one that I continue to hold on to today: Growth doesn't happen overnight. Salvation happens in a single moment of grace, but transformation—becoming more like Christ—is a lifelong process. It's called sanctification, the ongoing work of God in our lives as He shapes us into His image.

Paul speaks to this beautifully in Philippians 1:6:

"He who began a good work in you will carry it on to completion until the day of Christ Jesus."

This verse became an anchor for me as I wrestled with doubts and frustrations about my own growth. It was a reminder that God wasn't finished with me yet. The work of transformation didn't depend solely on my effort; it was something God was doing in me. And He had promised to complete it.

At the same time, I realized that growth wasn't entirely passive. While God is the One who transforms us, He calls us to partner with Him in the process. He invites us to take intentional steps of faith, to lean into His Word, and to cultivate habits that nurture our relationship with Him.

Looking back, I can see how God began to grow me, step by step, in those early days. It didn't happen all at once, and most of it didn't happen in dramatic or extraordinary ways. Some of the most significant growth came through small, faithful choices—moments where I simply showed up, sought Him, and allowed Him to do His work in me.

One of the first areas where I began to grow was in my understanding of Scripture. I'll never forget the evening I sat down with my Bible, feeling completely overwhelmed. I had no idea where to begin. To me, the Bible felt like a massive book of stories, laws, and teachings that I could never hope to fully understand. But someone had encouraged me to start with the Gospels, so I turned to Matthew and began reading.

At first, the words felt familiar but distant—stories about Jesus that I had heard before but never truly absorbed. Yet as I kept reading, something began to shift. The words started to sink deeper, as though God Himself was speaking directly to me. I was struck by Jesus' compassion, His authority, and the way He welcomed people—broken, flawed, and needy people—into His presence. His teachings challenged me, His love comforted me, and His truth began to reshape how I saw myself and the world around me.

Slowly, I started to see that Scripture wasn't just a collection of ancient words. It was alive. It was active. It was God's voice speaking to my heart, guiding me and revealing more of who He is. As I spent time in His Word, I began to hunger for it—not as an obligation, but as a lifeline.

Prayer was another area where I started to experience growth, though it didn't look the way I expected. Early on, I thought prayer had to be polished and formal—full of eloquent words and carefully constructed phrases. I thought if I didn't get it "right," God wouldn't hear me.

But over time, I began to see that prayer wasn't about impressing God—it was about being honest with Him. Some of the most powerful prayers I ever prayed were the simplest ones: "God, I don't know what to do. I need Your help." Or, "God, I'm struggling."

Those raw, unfiltered moments of prayer taught me that God doesn't need perfection. He wants my heart. Prayer became less of a religious duty and more of an open conversation with the One who knows me fully and loves me completely. It became a refuge—a place where I could bring my doubts, fears, and gratitude, knowing that He hears every word.

Another critical area of growth came when I learned the importance of community. For a long time, I had assumed faith was something personal—something just between me and God. But as

I began to build relationships with other believers in my church, I discovered how deeply God uses people to shape us and strengthen us.

In those early days, I was hesitant to let others in. I didn't want people to see my struggles or know about my doubts. I feared being judged or rejected. But as I started to open up, I found something unexpected: grace. I discovered that I wasn't alone in my struggles. I met people who had walked through similar seasons, people who were willing to encourage me, challenge me, and pray with me.

I'll never forget a conversation I had with a man named Mr. Harmon. I was in a season of doubt—wondering if I was doing enough, if I really belonged in God's family, if I would ever "get it right." Mr. Harmon, who had walked with the Lord for decades, listened to me pour out my heart without interruption. And then he simply said, "You don't have to have it all figured out. God's not finished with you yet."

His words were simple, but they brought me such comfort. He reminded me that this journey is about progress, not perfection. He reminded me that God is patient and kind, and He meets us exactly where we are.

I also learned that growth doesn't always feel dramatic or visible. Sometimes, it's slow and quiet—like seeds planted in the soil. Galatians 6:9 says, "Let us not become weary in doing good, for at the proper time we will reap a harvest if we do not give up."

There were seasons when I felt stuck, when I wondered if I was growing at all. But as I look back now, I can see the evidence of God's work in my life—the fruit of the Spirit slowly taking root: love, joy, peace, patience, kindness, goodness, faithfulness, gentleness, and self-control. I saw it in the way I responded with more patience than I had before. I saw it in my willingness to forgive and in the joy I experienced even in difficult circumstances.

If you're walking through a season where growth feels slow or you're wrestling with doubt, I want you to know this: God hasn't abandoned you. He's at work, even when you can't see it. Growth may not always feel exciting, but it's happening—one small step of faith at a time.

So, take heart. Keep seeking Him. Spend time in His Word, talk to Him in prayer, and surround yourself with people who will encourage and challenge you. Trust that the same God who began a good work in you will carry it to completion.

Paul's words in Colossians 2:6-7 offer this encouragement:

"So then, just as you received Christ Jesus as Lord, continue to live your lives in Him, rooted and built up in Him, strengthened in the faith as you were taught, and overflowing with thankfulness."

Growth after grace is a journey—one of becoming more rooted, more built up, and more like Christ. It's not always easy, but it's worth it. Because in the process, we not only discover who we're becoming, but we also discover more of who God is—His love, His patience, and His unwavering faithfulness to us.

Keep walking, step by step. He's with you every moment of the way.

THE JOURNEY

Chapter Fourteen: Living in the Power of the Spirit

Spiritual growth is not something we can manufacture on our own. For a long time, I thought it was. I believed that if I just worked harder, prayed longer, or read more Scripture, I could force myself to become the person I thought God wanted me to be. I approached my faith the same way I approached the rest of life: with grit, determination, and the relentless belief that my effort would be enough.

But no matter how hard I tried, I kept falling short. I would take one step forward, only to slide two steps back. I'd make progress for a season, only to find myself stuck in the same patterns of sin, frustration, and failure. The harder I worked, the more defeated I felt. I believed in God's grace for my salvation, but I still carried the burden of trying to change myself through sheer willpower.

What I didn't realize then was that spiritual growth isn't about striving harder—it's about surrendering deeper. The strength to change doesn't come from within me; it comes from the Holy Spirit. He is the source of power, transformation, and life that I could never manufacture on my own.

It took me years to learn this truth, and even longer to embrace it fully. The turning point came when I encountered a passage in Romans that stopped me in my tracks. I had read it before, but this time, it hit me differently.

It was Romans 8:11:

"The Spirit of God, who raised Jesus from the dead, lives in you. And just as God raised Christ Jesus from the dead, he will give life to your mortal bodies by this same Spirit living within you."

I read that verse over and over, letting the words sink in. The Spirit of God—the same Spirit who raised Jesus from the grave—lives in me? That was a reality I couldn't wrap my head around at first. I had been trying to change through my own strength when, all along, the power to grow and overcome was already within me, not because of anything I had done, but because of who God is.

That truth was like a lightning bolt to my heart. The Spirit wasn't just an abstract theological idea or a distant force. He was personal. He was alive. And He was in me.

Jesus had promised this. In John 14:16-17, He told His disciples:

"And I will ask the Father, and he will give you another Advocate to help you and be with you forever—the Spirit of truth. The world cannot accept him, because it neither sees him nor knows him. But you know him, for he lives with you and will be in you."

Jesus didn't leave us to figure life out on our own. The Holy Spirit is our Advocate, our Helper, and our Comforter. He doesn't just walk with us; He lives in us. And when we allow Him to lead, He empowers us to live lives of purpose, strength, and transformation.

This realization marked a shift in my faith. It didn't happen overnight—I'm still learning to rely on the Spirit daily—but it changed the way I approached my struggles, my growth, and my relationship with God.

For so long, I had carried the weight of trying to fix myself. I thought I could will my way into holiness. But the harder I tried, the more I realized I couldn't do it on my own. There was one struggle in particular that I fought for years—an old habit I knew wasn't honoring God. I resolved to break free time and time again, making promises to myself and to Him: "This time, I'll get it right." But every time I failed, I felt more ashamed, more defeated, and more unworthy of His grace.

One night, after another cycle of trying and failing, I fell to my knees and prayed a desperate, honest prayer: "God, I can't do this. I've tried everything, and I can't fix this on my own. I need You. Please, help me."

It wasn't an eloquent prayer. It was raw and simple. But it was the first time I truly surrendered—not just the struggle itself, but my need to control it. And in that moment, I sensed the Spirit's presence in a way I hadn't before. It wasn't a dramatic experience with flashing lights or audible voices, but it was real. I felt a peace wash over me, like God was saying, "I've got this. Lean on Me."

From that moment on, I began to approach the struggle differently. Instead of relying on my own strength, I turned to the Spirit in prayer. I asked for His help daily—sometimes hourly—and I trusted that He was at work in me, even when I didn't see instant results. Slowly, over time, I began to experience freedom. The chains that had felt unbreakable for so long started to loosen, not because I had become stronger, but because I was finally relying on the One who is strong.

That's the beauty of the Holy Spirit's work. He doesn't just help us "do better." He transforms us from the inside out. He changes our desires, renews our minds, and produces fruit in our lives that we could never produce on our own.

Galatians 5:22-23 describes this transformation as the "fruit of the Spirit":

"But the fruit of the Spirit is love, joy, peace, forbearance, kindness, goodness, faithfulness, gentleness and self-control."

These qualities aren't things we can manufacture through self-discipline or effort. They're the natural result of staying connected to the Spirit and allowing Him to work in us. As we surrender to Him, He produces this fruit in our lives—evidence of His presence and power.

For me, keeping in step with the Spirit has meant learning to listen for His voice in the small, ordinary moments of life. Sometimes, it's through Scripture—a verse that speaks directly to my situation.

Other times, it's a quiet nudge in my heart, prompting me to forgive, to speak up, or to reach out. The Spirit often leads us in ways that don't always make sense to our natural minds, but when we follow, we experience His peace, power, and provision.

I'll never forget the time the Spirit nudged me to reconcile with someone I had hurt in the past. Everything in me resisted. I didn't want to open that door or risk rejection. But the conviction was clear, and after much prayer (and hesitation), I took that step. It wasn't easy, but it brought healing I hadn't thought possible. That moment taught me that obedience to the Spirit, even when it's hard, always leads to life and freedom.

The Holy Spirit's power isn't limited to helping us overcome struggles. He also equips us to live boldly for God. In Acts 1:8, Jesus told His disciples:

"But you will receive power when the Holy Spirit comes on you; and you will be my witnesses in Jerusalem, and in all Judea and Samaria, and to the ends of the earth."

That promise is for us too. The Spirit empowers us to share our faith, to love others selflessly, and to live with purpose. He gives us the courage to step out in obedience, even when it's uncomfortable, and the strength to keep going when life gets hard.

If you're reading this and you feel stuck—if you're exhausted from trying to fix yourself or frustrated by your lack of progress—I want you to know this: you don't have to do it alone. The same Spirit who raised Jesus from the dead lives in you. He's ready to guide you, strengthen you, and transform you if you'll let Him.

The journey begins with surrender. It's saying, "God, I can't do this on my own. I need You." It's choosing to rely on the Spirit's power instead of your own.

Jesus didn't leave us to walk this journey alone. He gave us the gift of His Spirit—a gift that is personal, powerful, and life-changing. The Spirit is our guide, our comforter, and our source of strength. And He's available to you right now.

Take a moment today to pause, pray, and invite the Holy Spirit to lead you. Surrender your struggles, your plans, and your fears to Him. Trust that He is at work, even when you can't see it.

Because when you live in the power of the Spirit, you'll discover a strength that's not your own. You'll experience freedom, transformation, and purpose. And you'll begin to live the life God created you for—one step at a time, in the power of His Spirit.

"Since we live by the Spirit, let us keep in step with the Spirit." (Galatians 5:25)

Chapter Fifteen: Transformed Desires, Renewed Mind

When I first began my journey of faith, I believed that following Jesus meant trying harder—working to behave differently, fix my flaws, and follow a new set of rules. In my mind, transformation was something I had to manufacture. I assumed if I could just adjust my outward actions—speak better, think cleaner, and avoid sin—then I would finally become the person God wanted me to be.

I didn't realize it then, but I was approaching faith the way I approached everything else in life: with grit and determination. I thought it was up to me to make it happen. What I didn't yet understand was that God's work of transformation doesn't start on the outside; it begins in the deepest parts of who we are—our hearts, our desires, and our minds.

Paul says it perfectly in Romans 12:2:

"Do not conform to the pattern of this world, but be transformed by the renewing of your mind. Then you will be able to test and approve what God's will is—his good, pleasing and perfect will."

At first glance, the word "transformation" sounds dramatic and instant, doesn't it? But in my experience, transformation is far more subtle. It's slow, steady, and deeply intentional. It's not a surface-level shift—it's a work of grace that begins deep inside us and radiates outward. God doesn't just tweak our behaviors; He reshapes our desires and renews our minds so we become aligned with Him.

It took me a long time to understand that I couldn't change myself through sheer effort. The habits I wanted to break, the patterns I wanted to change, and the desires I wanted to overcome were far too ingrained for willpower alone to solve. I realized I didn't just need self-control; I needed God's power. I didn't need to "try harder"; I needed to surrender more fully.

For most of my life, I thought desires were fixed—unchanging, immovable parts of who I was. I thought, This is just who I am. These are the things I want, and they'll never change. I believed I had to fight against my desires rather than seeing them transformed.

Desires are powerful. They are the driving force behind our choices, our actions, and the way we live our lives. The world constantly feeds our desires, telling us that satisfaction comes through success, wealth, comfort, approval, or control. It convinces us that these are the things worth chasing, the things that will make us whole.

But the truth is, those desires will never fulfill us. They offer temporary satisfaction at best, leaving us restless and empty when they fail to deliver.

When we come to Christ, He doesn't just forgive us and leave us as we are—He begins to transform us. He changes what we want. He takes the desires that once pulled us away from Him—desires for selfish ambition, shallow pleasure, or fleeting approval—and replaces them with new desires that are good, pure, and life-giving.

Psalm 37:4 puts it this way:

"Take delight in the Lord, and he will give you the desires of your heart."

At first, I misunderstood this verse. I thought it meant God would give me whatever I wanted, like a wish-granting genie. But as I grew in my faith, I began to see the true meaning: when we delight in God—when we draw close to Him and allow Him to shape us—He transforms our hearts. Our desires start to reflect His desires. We begin to long for the things that bring Him glory and bring us joy.

For me, this transformation of desire was a gradual process. There were things I once chased with all my energy—approval, entertainment, and comfort that began to lose their grip on me. It wasn't that I suddenly stopped wanting those things overnight, but as I spent more time with God, something shifted. He planted new desires in my heart: a hunger to know Him more deeply, a longing to love others with greater selflessness, and a passion to live for His glory instead of my own.

This wasn't easy. Letting go of old desires felt like losing parts of myself, like giving up control. But I learned to trust that God's ways were higher than mine. And what I discovered was that His desires for me were so much better than anything I had wanted for myself.

The things I once thought would satisfy me—worldly success, admiration, ease—paled in comparison to the peace and purpose I found in pursuing Him.

While God was transforming my desires, He was also renewing my mind. The mind is a battleground. It's where we interpret the world around us, where we form beliefs about ourselves and about God, and where so much of the spiritual fight takes place.

For years, my mind was shaped by the world—by messages of fear, shame, and self-sufficiency. Whether it was through media, culture, or my own insecurities, I had absorbed countless lies about who I was and what I needed to be.

I believed I wasn't good enough. I believed my worth was tied to my success. I believed I had to earn God's approval.

But here's the truth: God's transformation of our lives begins when we allow Him to renew our minds.

Paul writes in Ephesians 4:22-24:

"You were taught, with regard to your former way of life, to put off your old self, which is being corrupted by its deceitful desires; to be made new in the attitude of your minds; and to put on the new self, created to be like God in true righteousness and holiness."

Renewing our minds means replacing lies with truth, fear with faith, and shame with grace. It's about choosing to see the world through God's eyes instead of our own.

For me, this process started with God's Word. At first, reading the Bible felt overwhelming. I didn't always know where to start, and I often felt like I wasn't "getting it." But the more I read, the more I began to see God's truth confronting the lies I had believed for so long.

Psalm 119:105 says:

"Your word is a lamp to my feet and a light to my path."

When I filled my mind with Scripture, I gave God's Spirit the opportunity to reshape my thoughts. Verses I had read a hundred times before began to take on new meaning. They reminded me of who I was in Christ: forgiven, chosen, and deeply loved. They gave me courage when I was afraid and comfort when I was weary.

Paul writes in 2 Corinthians 10:5:

"We take captive every thought to make it obedient to Christ."

Taking every thought captive became a daily practice. I learned to recognize when my thoughts didn't align with God's truth and to replace them with what Scripture said. When I felt unworthy, I reminded myself that I was made new in Christ (*2 Corinthians 5:17*). When I worried about the future, I clung to God's promise to work all things for good *(Romans 8:28)*.

This didn't happen overnight. Renewing your mind takes time and intentionality. But as I continued to lean into God's Word and listen to the Holy Spirit, my perspective began to shift. I started to see myself and the world the way God does.

As God transforms our desires and renews our minds, the evidence of His work begins to overflow into every area of our lives. We start to value what He values: loving others, pursuing justice, serving selflessly, and living with integrity. Our lives become a testimony to the power of His grace and the truth of His promises.

The change is often subtle at first. You might not even notice it happening. But over time, you'll look back and see how far God has brought you. You'll notice how your desires have shifted, how your thoughts have been renewed, and how your life has been realigned with His purposes.

Transformation isn't a destination; it truly is a journey. And as long as you walk with Him, God will be faithful to complete the work He has begun in you.

Chapter Sixteen: Overcoming Trials, Faith in the Fire

Faith feels natural when life is steady. When the sun is shining, prayers are answered, and everything seems to fall into place, trusting God feels almost second nature. It's in those seasons of peace, where provision abounds and the path is clear, that faith feels strong, simple, and undemanding—a quiet assurance that God is good, and all is well.

But faith is not truly tested in the easy days. It's in the moments when life shifts, when the ground beneath you begins to quake and the fires of trials blaze hot around you, that faith becomes more than an idea. It becomes your lifeline, the anchor that holds you when the flames threaten to consume everything you know.

The fires of life—trials, sufferings, and struggles—test not only the depth of our faith but also what we truly believe about God. Do we believe He is good even when life feels anything but good? Do we trust His presence when it feels like we're walking alone? Do we still cling to His promises when all our circumstances seem to contradict them?

These questions are not easy to face, but they are necessary. And the fire—painful as it is—has a purpose. Trials are not interruptions in God's plan for our lives. They are part of the plan. They are the refining ground where God works deeply within us, shaping us into who He created us to be. The fire reveals where our hope is truly anchored. It exposes what is temporary and strengthens what is eternal.

Jesus never sugarcoated this reality. He prepared us for it:

"In this world you will have trouble. But take heart! I have overcome the world." (John 16:33)

Trouble is inevitable in a broken world. The fires of life don't ask for permission to enter—they often arrive without warning. A sudden phone call changes everything. A relationship fractures. The weight of financial burden presses down. Illness appears, or grief comes like a tidal wave, leaving us struggling to breathe. At other times, the fire burns long and slow, wearing us down over weeks, months, or even years.

In these moments, it's natural to ask: Where is God in this? Does He see me? Does He care?

These questions do not make our faith weak—they make it real. I've been there. I've stood in the fire, overwhelmed and unsure, shouting those same questions into the silence. And yet, it's in those moments when I've also discovered this truth: God doesn't abandon us in the flames. He steps into the fire with us.

I learned this truth firsthand during the summer of 1982, a season I will never forget. That summer, I didn't just face a metaphorical fire—I stood in the middle of a literal one. It was a fire that changed me, not only physically but spiritually. It was there, in the heat and chaos, that I began to understand what it means to truly trust God in the fire.

My father had come to visit from Michigan, and the day before the fire, my cousin and I had been cutting a downed tree on the property. We mixed gasoline with 2-cycle oil for the chainsaw but made a careless mistake: instead of storing it in a proper, labeled container, we poured the mixture into an unmarked milk jug. It seemed harmless at the time—a small oversight with consequences we couldn't have foreseen.

The next morning, before anyone else was awake, my father went to stoke the coal-burning stove in my aunt's house. He reached for what he thought was coal oil to help the fire catch, but he grabbed the unmarked milk jug instead. I was asleep on a sofa bed just a few feet away when I was jolted awake by a deafening explosion.

The sight that met my eyes is one I'll never forget—my father, engulfed in flames. Panic and adrenaline took over. I jumped up, grabbed a blanket, and ran to him, smothering the fire as best I could before pushing him out the back door to safety. I yelled for my cousin, who had been sleeping in a back room, and then turned back into the house.

The fire was spreading quickly. Flames licked up the walls and rolled across the ceiling, filling the room with thick, black smoke. I could feel the heat pressing down on me, making it hard to think or breathe. For a moment, I froze in fear. Then, somewhere in the chaos, a memory surfaced—a fire safety commercial I'd seen as a kid. "When there's smoke, get low and crawl to safety."

That memory saved my life. I threw a blanket over myself, dropped to the ground, and began crawling toward the front door. The air was clearer down low, but when I reached the door, I realized the chain lock at the top had been latched. My heart pounded as I realized I would have to stand up, exposed to the flames, to unlock it.

I don't remember much of what I prayed—just a desperate cry for help—but somehow, I forced myself to rise. The blanket I had used for protection melted into my skin from the intense heat as I fumbled with the chain and yanked the door open. I stumbled onto the porch, jumped off, and rolled across the grass to extinguish the flames on my body.

Relief came when I saw my father and cousin outside, alive but shaken. Moments later, I learned that my aunt had already left for work that morning. She wasn't inside.

When I arrived at the hospital, the severity of my burns became immediately clear. Both of my arms were so badly damaged that the nurses couldn't find a vein for an IV. I barely registered what was happening as they worked quickly, eventually inserting the IV needle into my ankle—a detail I only pieced together later. From there, they immersed me in a large tub filled with ice and water to stop the burns from spreading further. The shock of the cold water against my raw, blistered skin sent a wave of pain so intense it's hard to put into words. It felt like every nerve in my body was screaming, and before I knew it, everything went dark.

When I woke up, I had no idea how much time had passed. Eleven days, they told me later. I was in the isolation ward, lying beneath a tent-like covering that had been carefully draped over the core of my body. My arms and shoulders, where the blanket had fused to my skin, were now unrecognizable—what had once been flesh was now a single, grotesque blistered surface. My body felt foreign, swollen and fragile, as though one wrong movement would cause it to shatter completely.

Those early days in the hospital were a blur—muffled voices of doctors and nurses, sharp smells of antiseptic, and the ever-present hum of machines monitoring my fragile state. Pain became my constant companion. Every movement, no matter how slight, set my nerves ablaze. Bandage changes, wound cleanings, and physical therapy sessions stretched on endlessly, each one a new ordeal that tested the limits of what I could endure. There were moments when the pain was so overwhelming that I slipped in and out of awareness, my mind retreating to shield itself from what my body was feeling.

In those long, silent stretches of recovery—when the hospital room felt cold and sterile, when the pain came in waves, and when sleep was my only escape—I had more time to think than I ever wanted. The "why" questions crept in, heavy and persistent. Why did this happen? Why did God allow it? What had I done to deserve this?

For a while, I wrestled with these questions, replaying the explosion over and over in my mind as if searching for some answer I had missed. I thought of the unmarked milk jug, the fire that spread so quickly, the sound of the flames consuming everything around me. I thought of my father's cries of guilt and anguish, the moments of panic, and the life-altering scars I now bore. It didn't make sense. None of it seemed fair.

But in the stillness—somewhere between the relentless pain and the quiet isolation—I began to sense something unexpected: God's presence. It wasn't loud or dramatic. It didn't erase the pain or bring instant answers to my questions. It was subtle, like a whisper. A sense of peace that didn't match my circumstances. A feeling of being held, even in the midst of my brokenness.

I realized that God hadn't abandoned me in the fire. He had been with me in the flames—guiding me when I couldn't see, sustaining me when I was weak, and protecting me in ways I couldn't fully comprehend. The fact that I had survived at all, when so much could have gone differently, was evidence of His hand. He hadn't stopped the fire from happening, but He had carried me through it.

In that hospital room, as I lay beneath the tent of healing, I began to see my suffering through a different lens. My questions didn't disappear, but they no longer carried the same weight. I realized that God was using this trial to teach me something profound: that His presence is not dependent on my circumstances. Even when life feels out of control, He is still sovereign. Even in my pain, He is still righteous.

The fire had taken much from me—my physical comfort, my sense of control, my plans for what life "should" look like—but it could not take God's presence. In fact, it revealed His presence in a deeper way than I had ever experienced before.

Those weeks in the hospital were a turning point. It wasn't just my body that was healing—my understanding of God was being refined, much like gold in the fire. I began to cling to verses I had heard before but never truly felt. One in particular stood out:

"When you walk through the fire, you will not be burned; the flames will not set you ablaze." (Isaiah 43:2)

The fire had burned my skin, yes, but it had not destroyed me. The flames had left their mark, but they could not take what mattered most. God had been with me, and He was still with me.

That realization didn't make the recovery process easy, but it gave me hope. And hope, I learned, is a powerful thing. Hope doesn't erase the pain, but it gives you a reason to keep moving forward.

It shifts your focus from what you've lost to what God is still doing.

In time, the physical scars began to heal, though they would always remain as a reminder of what I had been through. But more importantly, the fire had refined something deeper in me—a faith that was no longer dependent on life's ease or comfort. It was a faith forged in the fire, tested and proven, and held together by the unshakable presence of God.

If I learned anything during those weeks, it was this: God does not promise to keep us out of the fire, but He does promise to be with us in it. And sometimes, it's in the fire where we see Him most clearly. The flames that threaten to consume us are the very place where His faithfulness shines brightest.

No matter how overwhelming your circumstances may feel, no matter how intense the fire may burn, know this: God is with you. He sees you. He will not let the flames have the final word.

The fire that you are walking through—whether physical, emotional, or spiritual—can refine you, if you let it. It can strip away what is temporary and deepen your trust in the eternal. It can teach you to depend on God in ways you never had to before.

And when you come through it—because you will come through it—you'll find yourself changed. Not destroyed, but transformed.

Not weakened, but stronger. And you'll carry with you a testimony of God's goodness that shines all the brighter for having been through the fire.

"Not only so, but we also glory in our sufferings, because we know that suffering produces perseverance; perseverance, character; and character, hope." (Romans 5:3–4)

Hold on to hope, even in the fire. Because God is holding on to you.

THE JOURNEY

Chapter Seventeen: Bearing Fruit, The Evidence of New Life

The fires of life refine us, but they are not the end of the story. While trials may test and transform us, what emerges afterward is something beautiful: the evidence of God's work—fruit that reflects His grace, His power, and His presence in our lives. In the previous chapter, we explored how God uses fire to purify us, strip away what doesn't belong, and deepen our dependence on Him. Now we turn to what happens next: bearing fruit.

When gold is refined by fire, it doesn't just emerge purer—it shines brighter, reflecting the light around it. In the same way, the trials God leads us through are not just for our survival but for our growth. When we cling to Him in the fire, when we trust Him to carry us through, He doesn't leave us unchanged. He produces in us a new kind of strength, a renewed heart, and a transformed life. That transformation shows up in the fruit we bear.

The fruit of a tree is one of its most captivating features. It's not just evidence that the tree is alive and healthy; it's a gift that nourishes, sustains, and carries within it the seeds of future growth. Similarly, the fruit we bear as followers of Christ—our actions, our attitudes, our character—are a reflection of the life and transformation He has worked within us. And just like the fruit of a tree, it isn't meant for us alone. It is meant to bless others, to glorify God, and to point a watching world to Jesus.

But here's the truth: fruit doesn't appear overnight. It grows slowly, over time, through seasons of cultivation, pruning, and care. Sometimes it emerges in unexpected ways—often through circumstances that stretch us, challenge us, and teach us to depend on God.

When I first started walking with Christ, I thought bearing fruit meant trying harder. I believed it was about effort—working to be more loving, forcing myself to be patient, and doing my best to act "Christian" on the outside. I treated spiritual fruit like something I had to manufacture on my own.

But the longer I've walked with Jesus, the more I've realized that bearing fruit isn't about trying harder—it's about staying connected to Him. In John 15:5, Jesus makes this beautifully clear:

"I am the vine; you are the branches. If you remain in me and I in you, you will bear much fruit; apart from me you can do nothing."

A branch doesn't strain or struggle to produce fruit. It doesn't rely on its own strength or effort. It simply stays connected to the vine, and the fruit grows naturally as life flows from the vine to the branch. The same is true for us. The fruit of the Spirit—love, joy, peace, patience, kindness, goodness, faithfulness, gentleness, and self-control—grows in our lives as a natural result of staying connected to Jesus.

This connection happens as we abide in Him—spending time in His Word, seeking Him in prayer, worshiping Him, and walking in obedience to His leading. When we stay close to Him, the Holy Spirit works in us, producing fruit that reflects His character and His presence.

One of the clearest lessons I've learned about bearing fruit came during a season when I was working with someone who seemed to test every bit of patience I thought I had. This person was difficult in every sense—constantly negative, sharp with their words, and combative in almost every interaction. I did my best to remain polite, but inside, I was irritated, frustrated, and ready to snap.

At first, I handled it like I always had. I vented to friends, complained about how unreasonable this person was, and asked God to fix the situation—preferably by removing them from my life altogether. But God didn't remove them. Instead, He used them to reveal something about me.

One day, after another particularly tense interaction, I sat down and prayed out of sheer exasperation: "God, I can't deal with this person anymore. I don't know what to do." In the stillness that followed, God didn't say what I wanted to hear. Instead, He reminded me of His patience toward me.

How many times had I fallen short? How often had I pushed Him away or acted out of selfishness, yet still found Him faithful, patient, and kind? If God had extended such grace to me, how could I refuse to extend it to someone else?

That realization humbled me. I had been so focused on this person's faults that I hadn't asked what God wanted to do in me through this situation. So I began to pray differently. I stopped asking God to fix the other person and started asking Him to change me. I prayed for patience, kindness, and a heart that reflected His love.

It wasn't an instant transformation. There were still moments of frustration, and I had to remind myself to depend on God in those interactions. But over time, I noticed a change. My responses became softer, my tone gentler, and my perspective shifted. I started to see this person not as a problem but as someone carrying unseen burdens—someone God loved and cared for deeply.

Then, one day, this coworker opened up to me about the struggles they were facing—burdens I never would have guessed. That conversation changed everything. What had once been a source of tension became an opportunity for understanding, connection, and even ministry.

Looking back, I see how God used that season to produce fruit in me—patience, compassion, and humility. He didn't just change my circumstances; He changed my heart. And the fruit He produced through me became a way for Him to work in someone else's life as well.

The fruit God produces in us isn't just for our benefit. It carries within it the seeds for future growth—seeds that can impact the lives of others. When we bear the fruit of love, joy, peace, and kindness, we reflect the heart of God to a watching world.

Jesus said in John 15:16:

"You did not choose me, but I chose you and appointed you so that you might go and bear fruit—fruit that will last."

The fruit we bear has eternal significance. It opens doors for relationships, builds trust, and creates opportunities to share the hope we've found in Jesus. People may not always respond to sermons or arguments, but they can't ignore a life that radiates love, joy, and peace.

When we choose patience with a difficult coworker, kindness to a stranger, or faithfulness in the small, unseen moments, we plant seeds of faith in the lives of others. We point them to the One who is at work within us.

It's important to remember that bearing fruit is a process. Just as a tree goes through seasons—springtime growth, summer abundance, autumn pruning, and winter dormancy—our spiritual lives also have seasons. There will be times when growth is vibrant and visible, and there will be times when it feels slow or hidden.

But through every season, God is at work. He is the gardener who prunes us so that we can bear even more fruit. He is faithful to complete the work He has begun in us. Paul reassures us of this in

Philippians 1:6:

"He who began a good work in you will carry it on to completion until the day of Christ Jesus."

So, what does it look like to bear fruit in your life? It looks like love that serves, even when it's inconvenient. It looks like joy that endures through hardship, peace that calms the storm, and patience that waits with grace. It looks like kindness to those who least deserve it, faithfulness in the small things, and self-control that trusts God's timing and plans.

When we live this way, we don't just grow—we shine. Our lives become a testimony to the transforming power of Christ. We reflect His goodness to the world and glorify the God who is at work within us.

As Jesus said in John 15:8:

"By this my Father is glorified, that you bear much fruit and so prove to be my disciples."

If you long to bear fruit that lasts, start here: abide in Him. Stay connected to Jesus through prayer, His Word, and surrender. Trust

Him to do the work only He can do. And as you walk with Him, you'll find that He is faithful to produce fruit in your life—fruit that not only transforms you but also brings hope, healing, and new life to a world in need.

THE JOURNEY

Chapter Eighteen: The Mission, Called to Make Disciples

Trials refine us, and the fruit we bear afterward testifies to God's work within us. But the story doesn't end there. The fruit of our lives—the evidence of the Spirit's work—is never meant to remain solely with us. It is meant to overflow, planting seeds of hope, faith, and transformation in the lives of others. God doesn't refine and renew us just for our benefit; He equips us for something far greater. Every season of growth, every moment of refining, and every ounce of fruit He produces in us prepares us for the mission He has given to every believer: the call to make disciples.

This is the central purpose Jesus left with His followers before He ascended to heaven. It's not an optional assignment for pastors, missionaries, or the "spiritually elite." It is a call for everyone who has been saved and transformed by God's grace. The fruit we bear—love, joy, peace, and patience becomes a message in itself. It opens doors, builds trust, and allows us to reflect the heart of God to a world desperate for hope.

But stepping into this mission requires a shift in perspective. It requires us to see our lives not just as our own but as part of God's redemptive plan to reach others. The fruit we bear equips us for this mission, and the mission compels us to move beyond personal growth into something eternal: walking alongside others as they, too, discover the life-changing love of Jesus Christ.

For me, this truth came alive during the summer of 2009, when Joy and I attended a weeklong church camp in Vassar, Michigan, with several other families from our church. We had been looking forward to it for months. At the time, life felt like a whirlwind—filled with routines, responsibilities, and noise that left little space for spiritual rest. This camp, set on quiet grounds surrounded by lush fields and wooded trails, felt like an opportunity to recharge and reconnect with God and each other.

Each day began with a community breakfast—plates piled high with scrambled eggs, pancakes, and fresh fruit, the air filled with the warm sounds of laughter and fellowship. As the campfire crackled nearby, the conversations around the tables were as nourishing as the food, drawing us closer together as a community. From there, we made our way to the sanctuary, where the morning sunlight poured through the windows, casting a golden glow on the wooden pews. As voices rose in song, the simplicity of it all—the meals, the worship, the shared moments—stripped away life's distractions and left space for God's voice to speak deeply and clearly into our hearts.

Throughout the week, the theme centered on Jesus' words in Matthew 28:19–20:

"Therefore, go and make disciples of all nations, baptizing them in the name of the Father and of the Son and of the Holy Spirit, and teaching them to obey everything I have commanded you. And surely I am with you always, to the very end of the age."

It was a passage I had heard many times before, yet somehow, I had missed the personal weight of it.

One night in particular stands out. It was Missions Night; an evening Joy and I had been anticipating. As we walked into the sanctuary, we saw flags from around the world draped across the stage—a tangible reminder of the global mission God had entrusted to His church. The atmosphere was different that night—expectant, reverent, as if God was preparing to do something significant.

The speaker that evening was a man whose quiet demeanor carried a profound authority. After reading the familiar words of the Great Commission, he looked across the room and said:

"This mission isn't reserved for a select few. If you have been saved by God's grace, then you have been called to share that grace with others. Making disciples isn't optional—it's the very purpose for which you've been saved."

His words landed like a heavy weight in my chest. For so long, I had assumed the Great Commission applied to someone else—missionaries traveling to distant lands, preachers proclaiming the gospel to crowds, or those who were older, wiser, or more "spiritual" than I felt. But that night, something shifted.

I realized that the call to make disciples wasn't about qualifications. It wasn't about being perfect or having all the answers. It was about obedience. It was about saying yes to God's invitation to join Him in His work.

Over the rest of the week, we explored what it really means to make disciples, and what stood out to me most was this: it's not complicated. It doesn't require a program, a script, or a particular skill set. It's deeply relational.

Jesus modeled this for us in the way He made disciples. He didn't gather a crowd and hand them a manual. He called twelve men to walk with Him, to share meals, to learn from His teaching, and to witness His love firsthand. He invited them into His life, showed them what it looked like to follow God, and sent them out to do the same.

"Come, follow me," He said to Peter, Andrew, James, and John, "and I will make you fishers of men." (Matthew 4:19)

Those words reveal the heart of discipleship. It's an invitation to follow Jesus and to invite others to do the same.

At its core, making disciples is about sharing life. It's about walking alongside others, pointing them to Christ, and helping them grow in their faith. It's about being a witness—not an expert.

In Acts 1:8, Jesus said:

"But you will receive power when the Holy Spirit comes on you; and you will be my witnesses in Jerusalem, and in all Judea and Samaria, and to the ends of the earth."

A witness doesn't need to be eloquent or extraordinary. They simply share what they've seen, heard, and experienced. They tell their story of how God has worked in their lives, trusting Him to do the rest.

One of the greatest misconceptions I had about the Great Commission was that it required traveling to far-off places or doing something grand and extraordinary. But God showed me that the mission begins right where we are.

For Joy and me, that realization changed the way we saw our everyday lives. Making disciples wasn't about going to another country (although for some, it might be). It was about being faithful in the ordinary moments of life:

Sharing the gospel with a coworker during a lunch break.

Encouraging a friend who was walking through a difficult season.

Praying with a neighbor who needed hope.

Every interaction, every conversation, and every relationship became an opportunity to reflect the love of Christ.

At the heart of the Great Commission is love. Jesus said:

"A new command I give you: Love one another. As I have loved you, so you must love one another. By this everyone will know that you are my disciples, if you love one another." (John 13:34–35)

It's love that compels us to share the gospel. It's love that keeps us walking alongside others when it's messy or hard. And it's love that reveals the heart of Jesus to the world.

When Joy and I left camp that week, we did so with a renewed sense of purpose. We knew that making disciples wasn't about achieving some spiritual milestone or doing something extraordinary. It was about being faithful in the everyday moments of life.

We've learned that God doesn't call us to change the world on our own. He simply calls us to be obedient with what He has given us—our time, our relationships, our story. As we step into the mission, He does the rest.

The call to make disciples isn't just a task; it's a purpose that gives our lives eternal significance. It's a privilege to partner with God as He transforms hearts and brings people into His family.

The mission is bold. It's beautiful. And it's for you.

Chapter Nineteen: Strengthened in Service

The many trials we face in this journey don't just prepare us to bear fruit—they prepare us for a mission far greater than ourselves. God doesn't transform us so we can live comfortably on the sidelines. Instead, He equips us so we can step into the lives of others, pouring out His love, grace, and truth in a way that reflects Him. In the previous chapters, we explored the fruit that emerges from a life connected to Christ—evidence of His Spirit working within us. Now, we move to the natural outflow of that fruit: service.

Service isn't just one aspect of the Christian life; it's a reflection of the very heart of God. Jesus made this clear not just in words but in actions. In fact, His entire life and ministry were built upon serving others. He healed the sick, welcomed the outcasts, and fed the hungry. He modeled humility in its purest form—laying aside His divine glory to take on the form of a servant.

One of His most powerful lessons on service came during His final hours with the disciples. As the shadow of the cross loomed large, Jesus gathered His closest followers for the Passover meal. Knowing what lay ahead, He knelt down and did the unthinkable— He washed their feet.

"Now that I, your Lord and Teacher, have washed your feet, you also should wash one another's feet. I have set you an example that you should do as I have done for you." (John 13:14–15)

In that simple but profound act, Jesus redefined greatness. It wasn't about status, recognition, or power. Greatness, in His Kingdom, is found in service. The way up is down. The path to true significance is paved with humility and love.

But for many of us, serving doesn't always come naturally. It stretches us, challenges our comfort, and sometimes feels like a burden rather than a joy. I know this firsthand because I've been there—standing at the crossroads of my exhaustion and God's call to serve.

Several years ago, I found myself caught in a place in my journey where serving felt more like a duty than a delight. I was so focused on saying yes to every opportunity—volunteering at church, helping with ministries, signing up for everything—that I had unintentionally turned service into a checklist. I thought I was doing the right thing, but I was running on fumes. My well was empty.

One particularly cold Sunday morning in Flint, Michigan, I was scheduled to help at a local shelter that provided meals and warmth to the homeless during the brutal winter months. I admired the ministry and had committed to it weeks earlier, but when the day arrived, I sat in my car in the parking lot, gripping the steering wheel and fighting the urge to turn around.

I was exhausted. My body was tired, my heart was heavy, and spiritually, I felt completely drained. I remember whispering, "God, I don't have anything left to give. I can't do this today."

In that quiet moment, God brought to mind a verse I had read many times but never truly leaned into:

"My grace is sufficient for you, for my power is made perfect in weakness." (2 Corinthians 12:9)

It hit me: I didn't need to show up with strength of my own. I didn't need to have it all together. I just needed to be available and trust God to provide the strength I lacked. I whispered a simple prayer, asking Him to fill me where I felt empty. Then I got out of the car, walked through those doors, and let God do what only He can do.

What happened that day reminded me of something powerful: serving others doesn't drain us when we do it from a place of dependence on God. It strengthens us. As I worked alongside other volunteers—preparing meals, listening to people's stories, and sharing small moments of kindness—I felt my spirit being renewed. I had walked into that shelter on empty, but I walked out full. Full of gratitude. Full of peace. Full of the quiet joy that comes when we trust God to meet us in our weakness.

That day was a turning point for me. I began to see serving others not as a demand but as an invitation—an opportunity to encounter

God and be transformed in the process. Serving is not just about what we do for others; it's about what God does in us as we serve.

When we step into situations that stretch us—when we're asked to give when we feel we have nothing left—it forces us to rely on God in new ways. Service pushes us beyond our comfort zones and teaches us humility, compassion, and patience. It strips away self-sufficiency and draws us into a deeper dependence on God's strength.

It also changes the way we see people. When we serve, we begin to see others through God's eyes—not as inconveniences, interruptions, or problems to fix, but as people who are deeply loved by Him.

Several years later, I had another encounter that shaped my perspective on service even further. I was volunteering with friends Mark and Pam Amell at the Pilgrims Church in Detroit that ran a shelter and soup kitchen for the homeless. It was a chilly afternoon, and as the day wore on, I stepped outside for a break. I sat on a low brick wall across the street, watching people come and go.

That's when a man sat down beside me. He had come in earlier for a meal, and though he looked tired, his eyes carried a quiet warmth. We struck up a conversation, and soon he was sharing his story. He told me about losing his job, how he had been doing his best to support his family but kept running into closed doors.

I expected bitterness or anger, but there was none. Instead, he smiled softly and said, "God has been so good to me. He's given me everything I've needed, one day at a time."

Those words hit me like a lightning bolt. I sat there stunned, listening to this man—who had every reason to feel hopeless—talk about God's faithfulness with such trust and gratitude. I had shown up that day thinking I was there to serve him, but God was using him to teach me about what it means to rely on Him fully.

It was humbling and convicting. How often do I complain about what I lack, rather than recognizing God's provision? How often do I try to hold my life together on my own, when He's already promised to sustain me?

That conversation taught me something I've never forgotten: service is not just about giving—it's about receiving. When we serve, we allow God to teach us, stretch us, and reveal Himself to us in ways we might otherwise miss.

Jesus said, "Let your light shine before others, that they may see your good deeds and glorify your Father in heaven." (Matthew 5:16)

Service has a ripple effect. A simple act of kindness—a meal prepared, a word of encouragement, a helping hand—can open doors for conversations about faith. It can plant seeds of hope in someone's heart. It can point people to Jesus in ways we might never realize.

And it doesn't stop there. When we serve, we inspire others to do the same. Our willingness to say yes can spark a chain reaction of generosity, love, and compassion.

In the end, serving is not just something we do—it's who we are called to be. As followers of Jesus, we are His hands and feet in a world that desperately needs His love. When we serve, we reflect His heart. When we serve, we step into the mission He's entrusted to us.

So, let's approach service not as a burden, but as a privilege. Let's see it as an opportunity to encounter God, grow in faith, and point others to Him. Because when we say yes to serving others, we're not just meeting needs—we're being strengthened, renewed, and transformed by the One who first served us.

"Whoever wants to become great among you must be your servant." (Matthew 20:26)

May we embrace the call to serve with joy, humility, and faith, knowing that God is at work in and through us, every step of the way.

Chapter Twenty: Standing Firm in the Truth

As we continue this journey, having explored the mission of making disciples and the transformative power of serving others, we now arrive at a fundamental truth that holds everything together: standing firm in God's Word. Without this foundation, even the most faithful intentions, the most heartfelt service, and the deepest spiritual growth will lack direction and endurance. The Word of God is not merely a guide—it is the unshakable foundation upon which every aspect of our faith is built.

In a world that grows increasingly chaotic, where shifting cultural norms, conflicting opinions, and subtle deceptions compete for our attention, standing firm in truth is not optional—it's essential. It is the anchor that steadies us, the compass that directs us, and the light that illuminates our path. Without it, we risk drifting away, losing sight of who God is, who we are, and the purpose to which we've been called.

For me, the importance of grounding my life in truth became especially real during a season early on in my journey when my faith was quietly shaken. I had not turned away from God—I knew He was real, and I had seen His faithfulness firsthand. But doubt has a way of creeping in quietly, often through small cracks we don't even notice at first. My questions were subtle but unsettling. Some came from conversations with well-meaning people whose beliefs differed from mine. Others arose from my own fears and insecurities. What if I had misunderstood God's Word? What if my convictions were misplaced?

One evening, I came across an article online that seemed to call into question a fundamental aspect of my faith. The article subtly questioned the reliability and authority of Scripture, suggesting that the Bible—while valuable—was shaped by human hands and therefore subject to error and reinterpretation. It implied that parts of God's Word, particularly those concerning morality and truth, were outdated and needed to be understood in light of modern culture and evolving perspectives.

The question that arose from this was profound: How do I know where I stand is solid if I can't even tell what's true anymore?

The article's subtle twisting of Scripture made me wonder if the foundation I had built my faith on was as firm as I believed. It wasn't a blatant attack on Christianity; it was nuanced and carefully worded, which made it even more unsettling. For the first time, I was forced to confront the core of my faith and ask, Can I truly trust the Bible as the unshakable source of truth?

The problem was that it was almost true—it twisted Scripture just enough to make me pause. For the first time in a long time, I felt unsettled. I closed my laptop and sat in silence, wrestling with a question I had never fully faced: How do I know where I stand is solid if I can't even tell what's true anymore?

In my desperation, I reached for my Bible. It wasn't an act of habit—it was an act of surrender. I opened it to a passage I had read before but hadn't fully pondered:

"All Scripture is God-breathed and is useful for teaching, rebuking, correcting, and training in righteousness, so that the servant of God may be thoroughly equipped for every good work." (2 Timothy 3:16–17)

As I read those words, I felt clarity wash over me like a cool breeze on a sweltering day. Scripture is not just a collection of stories, rules, or moral lessons. It is God's voice—timeless, powerful, and unwavering. It is "God-breathed," meaning it originates from Him, carrying His very authority and character. Through it, He reveals Himself, teaches us, and equips us for every step of the journey He has called us to walk.

That night, I realized something I had been missing: My questions were valid, but I had been searching for answers in the wrong places. Instead of running to God's Word, I had allowed the world's voices to define my understanding of truth. I needed to stop treating the Bible like one voice among many and start letting it be the final word in my life.

One of the most dangerous lies we face as believers isn't an obvious one—it's the idea that truth is subjective. We live in a culture that celebrates personal truth: "You do you." "Live your truth." "Follow your heart." These messages may sound harmless, but at their core, they pull us away from God's absolute truth. When truth becomes relative, it becomes untethered, shifting with every whim, feeling, or cultural movement.

Paul warned about this in his letter to Timothy:

"For the time will come when people will not put up with sound doctrine. Instead, to suit their own desires, they will gather around them a great number of teachers to say what their itching ears want to hear. They will turn their ears away from the truth and turn aside to myths." (2 Timothy 4:3–4)

This passage is both sobering and prophetic. It's not merely about rejecting outright lies but about trading truth for something more comfortable—something that aligns with our desires rather than God's. This subtle exchange happens every day, and if we're not careful, we can fall into the same trap: following what feels good or sounds appealing instead of what is real and true.

So how do we stand firm when truth seems so easily distorted? The answer is surprisingly simple: We study the real thing.

Years ago, I read an analogy about how bank tellers are trained to identify counterfeit bills. They don't spend hours studying fake money. Instead, they study the real currency—its texture, its weight, its markings—so thoroughly that anything false becomes immediately obvious. The same principle applies to truth. The more time we spend in God's Word, the more deeply it takes root in our hearts, and the easier it becomes to recognize when something doesn't align with it.

This isn't about developing an academic knowledge of the Bible. It's about knowing God so intimately through His Word that His truth becomes the filter through which we see the world. When cultural trends shift, when opinions conflict, or when our emotions threaten to cloud our judgment, Scripture becomes our steady foundation—our unchanging anchor.

The journey of standing firm in the truth is not one we walk alone. God has given us the gift of community—the body of Christ—to encourage and sharpen one another. I think back to a young man I once met in our church. He was new to the faith, hungry to grow, but overwhelmed by the sheer number of voices and opinions competing for his attention. "How do I know what's true?" he asked me one Sunday morning. "There are so many different views—how do I sort through them all?"

I shared with him what I had learned: Start with Scripture. We don't need to chase down every argument or dissect every opinion. We simply need to know God's Word well enough to discern truth from falsehood. Together, we committed to meeting regularly, reading Scripture side by side, and allowing God to speak through His Word. Over time, I watched his confidence grow—not in his own understanding but in the unshakable truth of God's voice.

His journey reminded me of something important: We were never meant to navigate truth alone. When we walk alongside others, we strengthen one another, helping each other remain steadfast in a world full of confusion.

Standing firm in God's truth is not just about protecting our own faith—it's also about being a light to those around us. Jesus said:

"Let your light shine before others, that they may see your good deeds and glorify your Father in heaven." (Matthew 5:16)

When we live according to God's Word—when we hold fast to His truth with humility and grace—our lives become a testimony. People notice when someone is anchored in something unshakable, especially in a world where so many are drifting.

Standing firm doesn't mean we'll always have easy answers or that we won't wrestle with hard questions. But it does mean we know where to turn. It means we cling to the truth of Scripture and trust God to guide us when the path feels uncertain.

The truth of God's Word is not just a lifeline—it's a rock. It holds firm when everything else crumbles.

So, as we continue this journey, let's commit to staying rooted in God's Word. Let's seek it, study it, and live by it. Let's rely on the Holy Spirit to guide us into all truth and strengthen us when the world pulls us in other directions. And let's encourage one another, reminding ourselves and others of the unshakable foundation we have in Christ.

Chapter Twenty-One: Kingdom Mindset

The farther we walk in this journey, the more God opens our eyes to something greater. At first, we hold tightly to what's right in front of us—our jobs, our plans, our dreams—and we pour so much of ourselves into what feels urgent and tangible. But as we grow, God stretches our perspective. What once felt so monumental—our ambitions, our fears, even our struggles—begins to pale in comparison to the eternal scope of His plans.

In the previous chapter, we explored what it means to stand firm in God's truth, anchoring ourselves in what is real and unshakable. That foundation is essential, but it's only the beginning. God doesn't want us to stop there—He wants us to live differently because of it. The truth we cling to is meant to transform how we see the world and how we live each day. It's meant to lift our eyes from the temporary and root our hearts in eternity.

So, what exactly does it mean to live with a Kingdom mindset?

Living this way doesn't mean we ignore the realities of life here and now. Instead, it means that everything—our relationships, our work, our choices—becomes a reflection of God's eternal purpose. It's about realigning our priorities to match His, trusting that when His Kingdom comes first, everything else will fall into place.

For much of my life, I didn't see things this way.

I used to live with a narrow perspective, though I didn't recognize it at the time. Like so many people, I was focused on the here and now—building a good career, providing for my family, making plans for the future. None of these were bad things, but they consumed so much of my attention that my faith often felt like just one part of the puzzle instead of the framework holding it all together.

Then, life shifted in a way I hadn't expected. I lost my job as a CMM operator at the fixture shop where I worked in Romeo, Michigan. It happened suddenly—one day, the shop was buzzing with overtime and production deadlines, and the next, I was being handed a layoff notice.

At first, I felt numb. Then the questions began to flood in. How could this happen? What would I do next? What had all my hard work been for if it could be taken away so quickly?

In the days that followed, I scrambled to regain control. I spent hours sending out job applications, tweaking my resume until the words started to blur. I kept up appearances, but inside, I was unraveling. Losing my job felt like losing a piece of myself, because I had tied so much of my identity to my work. Without it, I felt unmoored, uncertain of who I was or where I was headed.

One night, as I sat at the kitchen table surrounded by newspapers and unanswered emails, I felt completely empty. The silence in the house only made the noise in my head louder. My sense of stability, which I had worked so hard to build, suddenly seemed fragile—like a house of cards that had come crashing down.

In that moment of quiet desperation I reached for my Bible, my reading brought me to Matthew 6, where Jesus talks about where we place our treasure:

"Do not store up for yourselves treasures on earth, where moths and vermin destroy, and where thieves break in and steal. But store up for yourselves treasures in heaven, where moths and vermin do not destroy, and where thieves do not break in and steal. For where your treasure is, there your heart will be also." (Matthew 6:19–21)

As I read those verses, it was as if God had put His finger on the very place in my heart where I had misplaced my priorities. My treasure—my focus, my time, my energy—had been invested in things that didn't last. My career, my achievements, my plans—these weren't bad things, but they had become my foundation, my sense of identity. And when they were stripped away, I realized how shaky that foundation had been all along.

That night, I saw the truth: My treasure wasn't meant to be tied to earthly success or temporary security. It was meant to be rooted in something eternal—God's Kingdom.

That moment marked a turning point for me. It didn't solve all my problems overnight, but it shifted my perspective in a way I couldn't ignore. God began to teach me what it means to live with a Kingdom mindset—to lift my eyes above the temporary and see life through the lens of eternity.

Living with a Kingdom mindset isn't about ignoring the realities of this world. It's about reordering our hearts. It's about choosing to trust that when we put God first—when we seek His Kingdom above all else—He will take care of the rest. Jesus made this clear when He said:

"But seek first his kingdom and his righteousness, and all these things will be given to you as well." (Matthew 6:33)

Those words aren't a promise that life will be easy. They don't mean we won't face hardships or uncertainty. But they are an invitation to trust. To believe that when God's Kingdom comes first in our lives, He will meet us in our needs, in our worries, and in the places where we feel most vulnerable.

So, what does this actually mean in our daily lives?

It means seeing work as worship. Whether we're teaching in a classroom, managing a business, or washing dishes at home, everything we do can be done as an act of worship to God. When we approach work this way, it becomes less about climbing a ladder and more about honoring Him with our effort and integrity.

It means investing in people over possessions. A Kingdom mindset reminds us that relationships matter more than accomplishments or material gain. The way we love others—our families, friends, coworkers, and even strangers—reflects God's heart to a watching world.

It means trusting God's provision. When we hold our plans with open hands, we find freedom from worry. We trust that God knows our needs and will provide in His time and His way.

It means redefining success. The world measures success by wealth, power, and status. But in God's Kingdom, success is defined by faithfulness. Did we love others well? Did we trust Him in our decisions? Did we point people to Him?

When we live with a Kingdom mindset, it changes everything. Our fears shrink, our purpose becomes clearer, and we begin to see life as part of something much bigger than ourselves. Every act of love, every word of truth, every moment of trust takes on eternal significance.

This doesn't mean life will always be easy. There will still be challenges, uncertainties, and seasons of loss. But when our hearts are anchored in eternity, we are no longer weighed down by those things. We can face them with courage, knowing that our lives are held in God's hands and that His purposes are far greater than we can imagine.

I think back to that night at my kitchen table, when I first realized how much of my life had been spent chasing things that didn't last. I didn't have all the answers that night, but I had clarity. God was showing me that my life wasn't meant to be about building my own kingdom—it was meant to be about investing in His.

That's the invitation He gives all of us: to live not for the temporary but for the eternal. To fix our eyes not on what we can see now, but on what is unseen and lasting (2 Corinthians 4:18).

So, let me ask you: Where is your treasure? What are you building your life around?

Living with a Kingdom mindset isn't about perfection—it's about surrender. It's about lifting our eyes, trusting God's provision, and allowing His priorities to shape our own. Each small choice we make to put Him first brings us closer to the life He's called us to live—a life that points to eternity and reflects His glory.

Because in the end, nothing else matters more.

Chapter Twenty-Two: A Witness to the World

Every believer carries a message—one far greater than ourselves, one that stretches beyond our own experiences, struggles, and limitations. This message is the gospel of Jesus Christ, the good news of salvation, redemption, and transformation. It's not something we've earned or crafted on our own; it's a divine gift, entrusted to us to share with the world. It's a message that can bring hope to the hopeless, heal the brokenhearted, and shine light into the darkest of places. But this message is not meant to stay hidden.

We are called to be witnesses—those who carry the light of Christ into a world that desperately needs it. This calling is not reserved for the extraordinary. It isn't limited to preachers behind pulpits, missionaries in far-off lands, or those with impressive platforms and persuasive words. It's for all of us. Jesus made this crystal clear when He said to His disciples:

"You are the light of the world. A town built on a hill cannot be hidden. Neither do people light a lamp and put it under a bowl. Instead, they put it on its stand, and it gives light to everyone in the house. In the same way, let your light shine before others, that they may see your good deeds and glorify your Father in heaven." (Matthew 5:14–16)

What an incredible responsibility—and privilege—that is. Light shines because that is its very purpose. It reveals, illuminates, and pushes back the darkness. As followers of Jesus, we carry His light—not because of who we are but because of who He is. And the purpose of that light is not to draw attention to ourselves, but to point people to Him, the true Light of the world.

For Joy and me, the journey of discovering what it means to live as witnesses began long before we ever set foot on a mission field. It started in simple moments—moments of faithfulness when God planted seeds in our hearts that we didn't even realize were there.

Do you remember the summer of 2009 we revisited in Chapter Eighteen? It was a turning point for us. That week at church camp in Vassar, Michigan, God stirred something in us that we hadn't fully recognized at the time. It was a week surrounded by fields, wooded trails, and humble cabins, but what made it sacred were the seeds God was planting in our hearts.

The speakers at camp shared powerful stories about people who had stepped out of their comfort zones to share the gospel—stories of families who loved their neighbors in simple but profound ways and students who carried their faith boldly into schools and communities. They challenged us to see the Great Commission not as an impossible command but as a personal invitation to join God's work. It wasn't about us or our abilities; it was about saying yes to the One who calls and equips.

We didn't leave camp with all the answers. We didn't have a grand plan for how we would live out the mission of being witnesses. But we did leave with open hearts and a willingness to say, "Lord, here we are. Use us." Sometimes, that willingness is all God needs to begin His work.

Five years later, in the summer of 2014, those seeds began to take root in ways we never expected. Joy and I joined a mission team bound for Johannesburg, South Africa, organized by Pastor Tim's church. The trip itself was the culmination of months of prayer, preparation, and trust. I'll never forget what Pastor Tim told our team before we left: "Remember, we're not going on vacation disguised as a mission trip. We're going to serve and glorify God."

The team was led by Brandon Dengler and his wife, Amber—a couple whose hearts for South Africa were deeply personal. Brandon had grown up there, and his father, Pastor Willie, led Mayfair Baptist Church just outside of Johannesburg that served the community through prison ministry, feeding programs, and outreach to children living in squatter camps. Together, Brandon, Pastor Tim, and Pastor Willie had carefully prepared the details of how our team would serve, and we were eager to step into the work God had prepared for us.

Johannesburg was a place of sharp contrasts—modern skyscrapers and bustling commerce stood just miles away from sprawling squatter camps where poverty gripped entire communities. During our time there, we worked in these overlooked places, the ones the world often forgets. We visited schools where children sang and laughed, despite having so little. We knelt in squatter camps, sharing the gospel with families who invited us into their small makeshift homes with generous hospitality. We entered prisons where men who had made choices that cost them their freedom sat quietly, listening to the message of God's forgiveness with tears streaming down their faces.

I will never forget the children's laughter as we sang songs of God's love. I will never forget the look in the eyes of prisoners as hope broke through their hardened exteriors. And I will never forget how humbled I felt as God showed me that His love knows no boundaries. It reaches across language, culture, and circumstances with a power that transcends human limitations.

Joy and I went to Johannesburg hoping to bring the light of Jesus to others, but we came home transformed. God taught us that the gospel isn't just something we share—it's something we live. It flows outward, drawing others to Him.

Three years later, in 2017, God stretched me again, this time calling me to lead a mission team to Quito, Ecuador. The task was different: we were there to help rebuild a Berean church that had been severely damaged by an earthquake. I felt the weight of leadership in a new way. I wasn't just part of the team; I was responsible for encouraging, guiding, and pointing others to Christ as we worked together.

The days in Quito were long and hot. We poured foundations, mixed concrete, and laid bricks—literally rebuilding what had been broken. The work was hard, but it felt sacred. Every bucket of cement we poured, every brick we laid, was part of creating a place where people would come to worship God for generations to come.

But as powerful as the work itself was, it was the people who taught me the most. The local believers we worked alongside had lost so much, yet their faith remained unshaken. Their joy and resilience reminded me of a truth I had seen in Johannesburg and now witnessed again: being a light for Christ isn't about what we have or what we've accomplished. It's about trusting Him in every circumstance and reflecting His love to those around us.

Those two trips—Johannesburg and Quito—were life-changing experiences, but they were only the fruit of something that began long before. They were the result of a simple, heartfelt willingness to say yes—to trust God even when we couldn't see the full picture. And here's the truth I've learned along the way: being a witness isn't defined by crossing oceans or undertaking grand, noticeable acts of service. It's not measured in miles traveled, platforms built, or recognition received.

Being a witness is about living faithfully right where you are.

When Jesus said, "You are the light of the world," He wasn't offering a suggestion or setting an impossible standard. He was making a declaration. If you belong to Him—if His Spirit lives in you—you are a light. It's not something we strive to be; it's something we already are because of Him.

The beauty of this truth is that His light goes with us wherever we go—into our homes, our workplaces, our neighborhoods, our schools. Whether it's across the globe or across the street, the light of Christ within us has the power to illuminate the darkest places.

Sometimes, the seeds God plants in our lives feel small—almost insignificant. A quiet conversation with a coworker. A simple act of kindness to a neighbor. A moment of prayer for a friend in need. It's easy to underestimate these moments, but God doesn't measure impact the way we do. Seeds of faith, no matter how small, can bear fruit in ways we can't yet see.

Those seeds might look like a listening ear when someone shares their pain. They might look like a patient spirit when tempers run high. They might look like extending grace where it's undeserved or sharing the story of what God has done in your life when someone needs hope. Every small act of faithfulness—every light we shine—reflects the character of Christ to a world searching for answers.

So let your light shine. Shine it boldly, even when you feel small or inadequate. Shine it joyfully, knowing that the source of your light is Jesus Himself. Shine it faithfully, trusting that God can use your obedience in ways you may never fully understand this side of eternity.

Because the life we've been called to is one of eternal significance. It's a life of purpose and hope, a life that points others to the One who overcomes the darkness. And that is a mission worth living for.

Chapter Twenty-Three: Walking Together, The Power of Accountability and Discipleship

Throughout this journey, I've come to understand that God rarely calls us to walk alone. While our faith is deeply personal, it is never meant to be private. The Christian life is designed to be lived out in community—encouraging, sharpening, and challenging one another to grow more like Christ. This truth became especially real to me during the mission trip to Johannesburg, South Africa—a trip that didn't just impact the lives of those we served but transformed my own life in a way I could have never anticipated.

It all started with a conversation.

We were nearing the end of our mission work in Johannesburg, after days spent pouring into others—ministering in schools, sharing the gospel in squatter camps, and serving alongside Brandon and his family. One evening, as the sun began to set and the team gathered for a time of fellowship and reflection, Brandon pulled me aside. His expression was serious yet kind, and I could tell this wasn't going to be one of our usual casual chats.

"I've been thinking," he began, "and praying about something I want to ask you."

There was a pause, not out of hesitation but out of intentionality. Then he said the words that would mark a turning point in both of our lives:

"Would you consider being my accountability partner?"

I was caught off guard, but in the best way. I respected Brandon deeply—his humility, his passion for serving others, and his steadfast love for the Lord were evident in everything he did. To have someone like him ask me to walk alongside him in this way was both humbling and honoring.

"Of course," I said without hesitation. "I'd be honored."

In that moment, my journey shifted. It was no longer just my journey—it became our journey.

That conversation in Johannesburg planted a seed that would grow into something far greater than I could have imagined. I didn't fully realize it then, but accountability is one of the most powerful tools God gives us for spiritual growth. It's not about checking boxes or pointing out flaws; it's about walking alongside someone with grace, truth, and love. It's about encouraging one another to stay rooted in God's Word, to live with integrity, and to pursue holiness even when the path gets difficult.

In James 5:16, we're told:

"Therefore, confess your sins to each other and pray for each other so that you may be healed. The prayer of a righteous person is powerful and effective."

Accountability isn't just about avoiding sin; it's about pursuing Christ together. It's about building trust and creating a safe space where we can be honest about our struggles, celebrate victories, and challenge one another to live in obedience to God's call.

Brandon and I began our partnership with a commitment to keep each other grounded. It wasn't formal or overly structured—it was real, honest, and consistent. We started by checking in regularly, sharing how God was working in our lives, where we were struggling, and what we were learning through Scripture. Over time, those conversations deepened. We opened up about our fears, our doubts, and the areas where we needed God's help most. We prayed for one another, encouraged one another, and pointed each other back to God's truth when we needed it most.

As the years passed, accountability gave way to discipleship.

Brandon's journey didn't stop in Johannesburg. God had a greater calling on his life—a calling to preach the gospel and shepherd His people. But discipleship doesn't just happen in sermons or ministry roles; it happens in the quiet moments of life. It happens in conversations over coffee, in shared study, and in the commitment to grow in Christ together.

Shortly after the mission trip, Brandon and I decided to take our next step together—we began attending theological classes. At first, it felt like a natural extension of what God was already doing in our lives. We both had a desire to deepen our understanding of Scripture, to be better equipped for ministry, and to know God more intimately. What I didn't expect, though, was how much studying together would strengthen not only our knowledge but our bond.

Those classes became more than academic exercises; they became opportunities to wrestle with truth, ask hard questions, and sharpen one another. There were days when we left class encouraged, feeling as though we had just unearthed a treasure of understanding from God's Word. There were other days when we left challenged—humbled by how much we still had to learn. But through it all, God was at work. He was growing us, stretching us, and preparing us for the roles He would call us to in His kingdom.

Brandon's call to preach became undeniable. I remember the conversations we had about it—his excitement, his humility, and his desire to faithfully obey whatever God had for him. There's something beautiful about watching someone step into their calling, and it was a privilege to see God's hand so clearly on Brandon's life.

Today, Brandon serves as the senior pastor of Bankers Baptist Church in Hillsdale, Michigan. I can't help but look back in awe at how God orchestrated it all—how He took a simple conversation in Johannesburg and turned it into something far bigger than either of us could have envisioned.

What I've learned through my journey with Brandon is that accountability and discipleship go hand in hand. They're not just for pastors, missionaries, or "spiritual leaders." They're for all of us. Jesus' command to make disciples wasn't optional; it was a central part of the Great Commission:

"Therefore, go and make disciples of all nations, baptizing them in the name of the Father and of the Son and of the Holy Spirit, and teaching them to obey everything I have commanded you. And surely I am with you always, to the very end of the age." (Matthew 28:19–20)

Being a disciple means being a learner—a follower of Christ who seeks to grow in His image. And making disciples means inviting others into that journey. It's not about having all the answers or being perfect; it's about being willing to walk alongside someone, pointing them to Jesus as you grow together.

Accountability is one of the practical ways we live this out. It creates space for honesty, vulnerability, and growth. It reminds us that we're not alone in this journey of faith—that God has given us one another for encouragement, support, and challenge.

Looking back, I'm reminded that the seeds God plants often grow in ways we can't predict. When Brandon asked me to be his accountability partner, I said yes, not knowing where that step would lead. What started as one small act of faithfulness grew into a shared journey of growth, learning, and obedience.

And that's how God works. When we say yes to Him—when we commit to investing in others, walking alongside them, and growing together in Christ—He multiplies our efforts. He uses our obedience to create a ripple effect that touches lives in ways we may never fully see or understand.

Perhaps someone in your life needs you to take that first step. Maybe it's a friend, a coworker, or someone in your church who needs encouragement, accountability, or discipleship. Don't underestimate what God can do through small steps of faithfulness. Your willingness to walk alongside someone else could be the beginning of a journey that changes both of your lives.

Brandon and I are still on this journey together. The conversations haven't stopped, and the accountability hasn't wavered. I'm continually grateful for the way God used our partnership to sharpen us both—to challenge us, to deepen our understanding of His Word, and to prepare us for His work.

Our journeys of faith are not meant to be walked alone. We need one another to grow, to stay the course, and to remain faithful to God's calling. So let's embrace this call to accountability and discipleship—not as burdens, but as invitations to be part of something eternal.

Because when we invest in one another, when we say yes to walking alongside a fellow believer, we step into the very heart of God's mission. We become part of His work of transforming lives, building His kingdom, and pointing the world to the hope found in Jesus Christ.

And there is no greater privilege than that.

THE JOURNEY

Chapter Twenty-Four: The Journey, A Life Transformed by Grace

As I sit here now at the age of 63, reflecting on the road I've traveled, I am struck by just how far God has brought me. It's almost impossible to reconcile the man I am now with the young man I was at 21—a restless wanderer, chasing after fleeting pleasures and superficial ambitions. Back then, I didn't have the faintest clue that God was quietly working behind the scenes, weaving threads of grace and redemption into my story. But as I look back, I can see it so clearly: His hand was always there, guiding me, even when I didn't recognize it.

My life has been anything but straightforward. There have been moments of overwhelming joy and others of deep heartache, seasons of abundant clarity and others of painful doubt. But through it all, God has remained constant—faithful, patient, and unrelenting in His pursuit of my heart. What I've come to realize is that grace doesn't always arrive in the form of an earth-shattering moment. More often, it unfolds in the everyday, in the slow and steady transformation that only God can bring.

The journey of faith truly began to take shape for me when Joy entered my life in 1986. Her name could not be more fitting, as she brought a light and sense of purpose into my world that I hadn't known before. At the time, I was far from the man God would eventually shape me to be, but He used Joy as a vessel to soften my heart and draw me closer to Him. In 1987, we were married, and even though I didn't fully grasp what it meant to build a marriage on the foundation of Christ, God was already at work, preparing us for the road ahead.

Marriage, as I would come to learn, is one of the most sanctifying experiences a person can go through. It requires selflessness, patience, and a level of vulnerability I wasn't prepared for at first. Joy and I faced our share of challenges—moments of tension, seasons of miscommunication, and times when we had to lean fully on God because we couldn't rely on ourselves. But through those trials, we discovered what it truly meant to love one another as Christ loves us.

One of the most significant milestones in our journey came in 2012, on our 25th wedding anniversary. That year, Joy and I renewed our vows in a ceremony that was as much a celebration of God's faithfulness as it was of our love for one another. Standing before our family and friends, I was overwhelmed by the realization of just how much God had carried us through. Those 25 years hadn't been perfect, but they had been filled with His grace—grace that sustained us in difficult times and made the good times even sweeter.

Becoming a father brought a whole new dimension to my journey. When Shalyn and Jared were born, I felt a mix of awe and responsibility unlike anything I had experienced before. I wanted to be a father who pointed my children to Christ, but more often than not, I felt painfully inadequate for the task. What I learned over the years, though, is that parenting isn't about perfection. It's about presence. It's about showing up every day, doing your best, and trusting God to fill in the gaps where you fall short.

Watching Shalyn and Jared grow into the people they are today has been one of the greatest joys of my life. Their hearts, full of kindness and wisdom, are a reflection of God's goodness. Seeing them step into their own journeys of faith has reminded me time and again that the work God does in us is never just for us. It's meant to overflow into the lives of those around us, leaving a legacy that points others back to Him.

And now, as a grandfather to Aurora and Scarlett, I feel the weight of that legacy even more deeply. Holding my granddaughters in my arms, seeing their innocent smiles and hearing their laughter, I am reminded of the faithfulness of God across generations. It's a humbling thing to know that the choices I make today—the way I live, love, and serve—will ripple into the lives of those who come after me.

But while I treasure the visible blessings of marriage, fatherhood, and family, I know that the greatest transformation God has worked in my life has happened in the quiet places of my heart. It hasn't been a quick process, nor has it always been easy. God has patiently refined me, using both joyful moments and painful ones to mold me into the man He created me to be.

One pivotal moment in that journey came during our mission trip to Johannesburg. When Brandon asked me to be his accountability partner, I thought I was simply agreeing to walk alongside a friend in faith. But what I discovered was that accountability is a two-way street. Through our conversations, prayers, and shared struggles, God revealed to me the power of vulnerability, encouragement, and mutual growth.

That relationship became a living example of what discipleship is meant to be—two people walking together, sharpening one another, and pointing each other back to Christ. It reminded me that faith was never meant to be a solo journey. We need each other. God uses the people He places in our lives to challenge us, encourage us, and draw us closer to Him.

At 63, I can say with confidence that God is not finished with me yet. Philippians 1:6 has become a cornerstone of my faith:

"Being confident of this, that he who began a good work in you will carry it on to completion until the day of Christ Jesus."

This verse is a reminder that the journey of faith is ongoing. It's not about arriving at some final destination or achieving a level of perfection. It's about continuing to walk with God, trusting Him to lead and transform us every step of the way.

Chapter Twenty-Five: The Journey Continues

Dear Reader,

As you've walked through these pages with me, reflecting on how God has moved in my life, my hope is that you've also been reflecting on your own journey. Because while this book may be coming to an end, your story is still unfolding.

The journey of faith doesn't end with a milestone reached, a problem solved, or even a book completed. It continues—step by step, day by day—as long as there is breath in our lungs and purpose in our hearts. And let me remind you: there is a purpose for your life.

If there's one thing I've learned, it's that God is always at work, even when we can't see it. His plans are higher than ours, His timing perfect, and His love unshakable. There were so many times in my life when I doubted, when I questioned, and when I couldn't see how He could possibly bring good out of a situation. But looking back now, I see His fingerprints everywhere.

I hope that as you close this book, you'll take a moment to reflect on your own story. Where has God been faithful? Where has His grace carried you? And where is He calling you to trust Him more deeply?

The road ahead may be uncertain, but it is full of promise. My prayer for you is simple: Keep walking. Keep trusting. And let the light of Christ shine through you.

The journey continues.

In Christ,

Michael McCullough

THE JOURNEY

Made in United States
North Haven, CT
12 January 2025